Meaningful Living

MEANINGFUL

LIVING

Paul H. Dunn

Illustrations
by
Richard L. Gunn

BOOKCRAFT
Salt Lake City, Utah
1968

LIBRARY OF CONGRESS CATALOG CARD NUMBER 68-28761

FIRST PRINTING, 1968

LITHOGRAPHED BY
PUBLISHERS PRESS

SALT LAKE CITY, UTAH
UNITED STATES OF AMERICA

DEDICATION

To my mother, Geneve R. Dunn, and to my brothers, Robert E. and N. David, for their influence in making the gospel meaningful and practical and an enjoyable "way of life."

CONTENTS

MEANINGFUL LIVING

Perhaps more articles and books have been written on the life and teachings of the Savior than on any other subject. This is as it should be, for no other life has influenced the world quite like his. Yet, there are those who marvel at his coming, his contributions, his divine sacrifice, and see little or no relationship between what he is and what he taught and their own lives.

People everywhere need to realize that Christ was as much interested in the home and the carpenter shop as he was in the establishment of the Church, that when he adivsed folks to live according to certain divine principles, he was not attempting to force them to obey the demands of an arbitrary God. Instead he was revealing to them the great fundamental laws of life, which make for happiness and success in this life and which prepare one for life eternal.

He said that he had come not as a judge, but as a representative of a loving, all-wise Heavenly Father to show us how to have life and have it in abundance. He had never built an automobile, coached a baseball team, or argued a case in court. But he had lived gloriously. In the great seething, boiling, tumultuous laboratory of experience he had gone back to the sources and had found there those eternal elements, the observanc of which would assure, and the neglect of which would prohibit, successful living. He spent a considerable portion of his time in teaching and illustrating those laws of life.

Every principle of the gospel that he gave is well known today. In fact, most if not all of these have already been adopted and made the basis of good business and social ethics. In many cases the leaders who use and teach these principles either do not know they came from our Lord or do not see any reason why he should be given the honor. The result is that many of the very people who have been led to accept the ethical standards of Jesus, at the same time, and, because of their lack of proper understanding, display little or no interest in the Divine Sonship of the Christ.

The purpose of this book, therefore, is to win for Jesus something of the allegiance that he deserves in the affairs of our everyday lives. We shall try to accomplish this purpose by organizing some of the divine principles he taught under twelve topics based primarily on his Sermon on the Mount. The author alone is responsible for the contents of this volume; they represent his interpretation of what the Savior meant when he taught the people of Palestine and those who inhabited the Americas.

I should like to add that this book is written, not so much for the highly trained Biblical scholar, as for the busy "man of the street," the "housewife in the kitchen," and the "struggling student" — for the person who is truly desirous of building a successful life but who has not seen the relationship between such accomplishment and the principles of Jesus.

Such an effort is the contribution of many. I am indeed indebted to my able secretary, Quaila Newren, for her devotion to this cause and for the many extra hours of typing the manuscript. A special thanks to Velma Harvey for proofreading the text; to Marvin Wallin and his staff for their many helpful suggestions. Once more, Richard Gunn has displayed his marvelous talents by his wonderful illustrations. I am particularly indebted to my father-in-law, Dr. C. F. Cheverton, whose own life and teachings did much to inspire the contents of this volume. Finally, to my wife, Jeanne, and my daughters, Janet, Marsha, and Kellie, I am eternally indebted for the encouragement and support they give.

—Paul H. Dunn
June 1968

REFLECTIONS ON THE OPEN MIND

Some people grow with responsibility, others just swell.

—STANSIFER

Everybody is ignorant, only on different subjects.

—WILL ROGERS

Every man has a right to be conceited until he is successful.

—DISRAELI

The less people speak of their greatness, the more we think of it.

—BACON

A high brow is one whose learning has outstripped his intelligence.

—VINCENT MASSEY

True humility, the highest virtue, mother of them all.

—TENNYSON

CHAPTER 1

KEEP AN OPEN MIND

Several years ago I came across a letter to my father-in-law, who was at that time a college president. The letter was from a teacher desiring a position on the college faculty. The applicant wrote as follows:

Dear Sir:

Notified May 21st that financial stress led me out here without disgrace. Late comer on faculty. Teach almost anything in modern French, German, and Spanish language. Literature. Courses for teaching scientific material and phonetics. Have made 31 public addresses since last January 1st. Have taught in three high schools, one state teacher's college, two state universities, and three denominational colleges. War, pestilence, famine, not inefficiency, make changes necessary.

I keep sane by hobby of music, playing flute, baritone, bass, also horns, clarinet, and cello. Can direct and lead chorus, bands, or orchestras, including the á cappella choir work which is now so popular. Have taught cello for years and can instruct in all band instruments.

Keep well by physical education. Have long taught and can still instruct as sideline in corrective exercises, floor activities in gymnasium, light apparatus, heavy German gymnastics, and swimming. Health lecturer, used repeatedly for institute work for teachers. Prefer teaching to research though keep up advanced study. Taught high school administration during seven summer sessions. Teacher of German this summer for the third time. Correspondence invited. Scholastic record enclosed.

Respectfully yours,

While the letter suggests the writer to be a man with

13

much confidence, the personal interview which followed
proved it was sheer conceit. If you were selecting a person for some important work, would you choose an egotist such as the author of the above letter? Or would you
prefer a person who realizes that there are a few things in
life that he does not know?

Dale Carnegie has said that more people lose their
jobs because of bad manners and unattractive personalities than for any other reason. In a survey of employees
who were dismissed from seventy-six different firms, only
ten percent, Carnegie reported, lost their jobs because
they lacked mechanical skills. Ninety percent were not
suitable because of poor character traits.

"Step aside! I want to walk where you're standing."

A prominent educator who has also done considerable work as a personnel director says that the worst fea-
tures of such people's attitudes are "pure, undefiled
egotism" and an unwillingness to listen to others and to
learn from them. "They want to tell the boss where to
head in. They are not willing to obey orders. They have
not learned that in life there are certain things that are
not debatable."

Even a college education cannot overcome the weakening effects of false pride. Note the case of a business corporation that chose one hundred college graduates, trained them in their work, and sent them out—only to see practically all of them fail. When asked the reason for the graduates' failures, the president of the corporation said, "They knew too much." When asked if his company would stop using college graduates, the president replied, "No, but we shall wait until they have been out of school for at least a year, so they will have had a chance to mellow."

Writing on the positive side of the problem, Bruce Barton says, "When we are through changing, we're through." The world's greatest men have been open-minded throughout their lives. Consider Benjamin

Franklin, how eagerly he sought new ideas even in his old age. Bacon and Pasteur were constantly seeking new truths. On his deathbed the great astronomer Laplace said, "What we know is nothing; what we have to learn is immense." "The secret of genius," as Carlyle has said, "Is to carry the spirit of childhood into old age."

LaoTsze, ancient Chinese teacher, counseled his students with these words: "Be gentle and you can be bold; be frugal and you can be liberal. Avoid putting yourself before others and you can become a leader among men." In popular phraseology another writer has said, "You cannot push yourself ahead by patting yourself on the back."

Isn't that what the Savior taught? "Blessed are the poor in spirit who come unto me." (Matt. 5:3, and 3 Nephi 12:3.) Greek scholars tell us that the word which has been translated "blessed" means almost the same as our English word "happy." Jesus came that we might have life and that we might have it more abundantly. (John 10:10.) He would help each of us to be happy. He would show us how to make the best use of all our God-given talents. He wants us to be successful in our vocations and accomplish every worthy purpose of our lives. To help us do this, he gave us as a starting point the first step of the upward climb—*Humility.* "Blessed are the poor in spirit who come unto me, for theirs is the kingdom of heaven. Blessed are the meek: for they shall inherit the earth." (Matt. 5:3,5, and 3 Nephi 12:3,5.)

These beatitudes are not threats from the Lord; they are statements of basic laws of life. A mind swollen with false pride cannot be easily opened to receive new truth. In a world that changes every day, each hour revealing new truths, the closed mind is destined to mediocrity.

As one clever wit has said, "Some people are buried

at seventy-five who were dead at thirty." Some teachers, lawyers, doctors, musicians, men in business and other professions, who have the natural ability to achieve great heights in their vocational work, nevertheless gradually drift into the background for the simple reason that they cannot see the need of constant growth. They think they have a corner on truth. They have broken the law of humility, and the law of humility is slowly but relentlessly breaking them.

One of the chief requisites for advancement in the business or professional world is willingness and ability to meet the needs and desires of one's fellow men. Jesus knew this. Dale Carnegie and others who have written on vocational success have discovered it.

One way not to get a head!

No matter how egotistical one may be himself, he does not respond favorably to the same quality in others. Blessed are the egotists, for by their false pride and know-it-all spirit they shall gain the love and appreciation of all men. Is it necessary to argue against such a statement? Will any sensible man or woman have the courage to teach such a doctrine and attempt to prove it by human experience? No wonder, therefore, that Jesus laid down as the first principle for successful living (vocationally as well as in every other sphere), blessed are the meek, the humble, the open-minded and the teachable—for they are the ones who shall inherit the earth.

Does the same principle apply to one's religious life? Jesus claimed it would, and he gave a wonderful example of the operation of that law. Two men, he said, went up into the temple to pray, one a Pharisee, the other a publican. (Luke 18:10.) Let us not forget they went into the temple *to pray*. If we neglect those two words, we are likely to miss the point of the entire story.

> The Pharisee stood and prayed thus . . . God, I thank thee, that I am not as other men are, extortioners, unjust, adulterers, or even as this publican.
> I fast twice in the week, I give tithes of all that I possess.
> And the publican, standing afar off, would not lift up so much as his eyes unto heaven, but smote upon his breast, saying, God be merciful to me a sinner.
> I tell you, this man went down to his house justified rather than the other . . . (Luke 18:11-14.)

Not an extortioner nor unjust, the Pharisee did not rob widows nor did he attempt to crush his weaker competitors. He paid good salaries and gave good measure. At almost every point, he was a better man than the publican. Yet he did not go away justified. His "prayer" had been no more than a boastful listing of his own good qualities and had shown no evidence of a desire for spiritual growth.

When we sang "Carry on", he did.

The publican, though an unjust tax collector, recognized his weaknesses and opened wide his soul to let the Spirit of God have its way with him. Jesus said, "I tell you, this man went down to his house justified rather than the other: for every one that exalteth himself shall be abased; and he that humbleth himself shall be exalted." (Luke 18:14.)

Jesus did not say that the publican was the better man; nor did he contend that the publican would be more favorably received into the kingdom of heaven. The point Jesus made was that although the two men had come to the temple to pray, only one of them, the publican, offered an acceptable prayer. Granted, the Pharisee was a highly respected man; however, he received no benefit from his prayer because he approached

God with a closed mind and with a feeling of self-sufficiency. The publican, on the other hand, petitioned God with an open mind and a contrite heart and benefited spiritually from his prayer.

Have you ever had someone ask you for advice and then spend all of your time attempting to prove that his own ideas were right? If so, how did you feel? And how much good would your advice do in such a situation? You cannot help a person who does not want to be helped and who does not see the need of being helped. God did not help the Pharisee because the self-righteous egotist would not give him a chance.

The only reason that God does not help us to develop more likeable personalities and more beautiful charac-

Fat chance of meeting "down to earth" problems.

ters, to become more successful workers in his kingdom, is that we do not ask with open minds and willing hearts. Most of us have been sufficiently earnest in repeating the first part of the publican's prayer: "Lord, be merciful unto me." We need not expect to get good results until we can place an equally sincere and serious emphasis on the rest of the petition: "Lord, be merciful to one who needs spiritual growth."

Augustine was once asked what he considered to be the first word in the Christian philosophy of life. He replied, "Humility." And the second? "Humility." The third? "Humility."

Jesus said, "Except ye be converted, and become as little children, ye shall not enter into the kingdom of heaven." (Matt. 18:3.) The same may be said about the kingdoms of science, music, law, sports, or business. "Except ye become as little children," except you realize your own weakness and with open, teachable minds go in search of new facts and added truths, "ye shall not enter into the kingdom."

Moses, the greatest leader of early Hebrew history, strong of body (Ex. 2:11-12), mind, and soul, was a natural leader of men. Yet so humble a spirit was he, that his people said, "Moses was very meek, above all the men which were upon the face of the earth." (Num. 12:3.)

When first called to serve God, Jeremiah protested, "Lord God! behold, I cannot speak: for I am a child.

"But the Lord said unto him, Say not, I am a child: for thou shalt go to all that I shall send thee, and whatsoever I command thee thou shalt speak." (Jer. 1:6-7.) Gaining confidence, not from any recognized power of his own, but from the promise of the Lord unto him, Jeremiah became a courageous, brilliant statesman and prophet of God, considered by many to be the most forceful and influential in the Old Testament.

Not solely through his teaching, but because of his matchless power of leadership and his divine calling, Jesus was literally the greatest of all leaders ever to walk upon the earth. Taking little glory to himself, he said to those who would compliment him, "Why callest thou me good? there is none good but one, that is, God." (Matt. 19:17.)

Paul, one of the most outstanding apostles of his time, was highly educated and proud of his Roman citizenship. Yet he spoke of himself as a weak specimen of humanity and chief among the sinners. (Rom. 7:19; I Tim. 1:15.)

Sir Isaac Newton, discoverer of the law of gravity, declared in sweet humility, "I do not know what I may appear to the world, but to myself I seem to have been only a boy playing by the seashore and diverting myself in now and then finding a smoother pebble or a prettier shell than ordinary, while the great ocean of truth lay undiscovered before me."

Abraham Lincoln, tall, sun-crowned man of the ages, frankly admitted to his critics that he may have been the very fool of whom they spoke. When condemned for putting into his presidential cabinet a man who thought himself to be superior to the president, Lincoln replied that if he knew others of the same caliber he would gladly put all of them in his cabinet.

George Washington, a wealthy man in rags, knelt with great humility and power at Valley Forge to seek the help of his Heavenly Father. Gladstone, later English prime minister, ran away for days at a time in order to get better control of himself and to search for unlimited knowledge of the divine. Along with leaders in science, medicine, and economics, our greatest university and college teachers frankly and openly admit their ignorance in the presence of unsolved problems.

In light of such noble and successful personalities as Benjamin Franklin, Sir Francis Bacon, Laplace, Carlyle, LaoTsze, George Washington, and Gladstone, let one who occasionally feels haughty and arrogant remember—call it theology, ethics, or just good common sense—that the principle of humility is valid. By following it, one can build a happier, more successful life. "Blessed are the poor in spirit who come unto me, for theirs is the kingdom of heaven . . . Blessed are the meek (those who are willing to grow, who through their democratic spirits are able to win the love and appreciation of others, and who with repentant spirits are anxious for God's criticism and help), for they shall inherit the earth."

REFLECTIONS ON KEEPING YOUR
ENERGIES PROPERLY FOCUSED

There is but one failure; that is, not to be true to the very best one knows.

—CANNON FARRAR

Speed becomes a substitute for direction.

—RUFUS JONES

Nothing in the world can take the place of persistence. Talent will not—genius will not—education will not —persistence and determination alone are omnipotent.

—CALVIN COOLIDGE

One of the great crimes which shortens life is indifference. The two most fatal phrases and the most common are: What's the use? and Why should I?

—CHAUNCEY M. DEPEW

No man is worth his salt who is not ready at all times to risk his body, to risk his well-being, to risk his life, in a great cause.

—THEODORE ROOSEVELT

CHAPTER II

KEEP YOUR ENERGIES
PROPERLY FOCUSED

About two miles from our former home, the framework of a house stood unfinished for several years. It was beautiful. It was in a very beautiful location. The plan of the house was interesting, and the material out of which the framework had been built seemed quite satisfactory.

As I continued to drive past the house month after month on my way to work, I noticed that the color of the lumber was gradually changing—first a faded yellow, then a darker yellow—light brown, then a darker brown—until at the close of the first year the framework appeared to be almost black.

Not only was the color changing, but with each passing day the skeleton of the unfinished house became more articulate until one day it actually seemed to speak to me. So challenging was its message, I know I shall never forget it. Like the voice from across the centuries, the blackened structure asked, "Which of you, intending to build a tower, sitteth not down first, and counteth the cost, whether he have sufficient to finish it? Lest haply, after he hath laid the foundation, and is not able to finish it, all that behold it begin to mock him, saying, This man began to build, and was not able to finish." (Luke 14:28-30.)

The message was being hurled directly at me and, I think, at all others who have sworn, regardless of cost, to build a completed life. Have we stood by this promise, whether the houses of our lives were large or small? Are our lives each day completed structures? Or has the tempting challenge of the crowd, the worries of depressing moments, caused us to become slack in our work? Do our lives now stand before the world as half-finished skeletons of the beautiful houses we had sworn to build?

The voice continued to speak. "What king, going to make war against another king, sitteth not down first, and consulteth whether he be able with ten thousand to meet him that cometh against him with twenty thousand? Or else, while the other is yet a great way off, he sendeth an ambassage, and desireth conditions of peace. So likewise, whosoever he be of you that forsaketh not all that he hath, he cannot be my disciple . . . He that hath ears to hear, let him hear." (Luke 14:31-33, 35.)

This voice of warning suggests Jesus' second principle of successful living. If we really want to build well, the first thing to do is to admit our weaknesses and need for development. We must be humble, open-minded, repentant. We must be poor of spirit and come unto him. We must be willing to mourn. We must be meek. But we must not stop there. Having admitted our present incompleteness, the next step is to put everything we have into the development of a great life. "And blessed are all they who do hunger and thirst after righteousness, for they shall be filled with the Holy Ghost." (3 Nephi 12:6, and Matt. 5:6.) "Seek ye first the kingdom of God, and his righteousness; and all these things shall be added unto you." (Matt. 6:33, and 3 Nephi 13:33.) Once again, the principle Jesus advocates is truly as old as the hills. Other things being equal, he intimates that we get what we seek if we seek it diligently enough.

Someone has said, "The longer I live, the more deeply I am convinced that that which makes the difference between one man and another, between the weak and the powerful, the great and the insignificant, is energy, invincible determination, the purpose once formed and then death or victory." Mark Twain felt much the same and expressed himself in this way, "If I were heathen, I would build a statue to energy and fall down and worship it."

When Sir John Hunt stood at the foot of Mount Everest, he did not expect his team of mountain climbers to reach its summit by some sort of magic or in one leap. He had mapped the climb by stages, one day at a time. Each day the men ascended as far as he had planned for that day. The morning that two members of his party, Hillary and Tenzing, finally stepped upon the summit was the climax of many days' efforts. The last step was the crowning one of many arduous steps to the top.

What you set out to do may not be as difficult or spectacular as climbing Mount Everest, but you must apply the same principle. There is no magic, no sudden leap that will carry you to your goal. You must go step by step, with full energy focused on the end you seek.

A friend of mine told me the following story:

> Some years ago a young man knocked on my door in Los Angeles. His clothes were threadbare, and his shoes were cracked. Poverty was written all over him. My first thought was that he wanted a handout. But something about him immediately drove that idea away. I invited him in and began to talk to him.
>
> "I'm going to be a doctor," he said. "I wondered if you could help me get a job to pay my expenses for medical school."
>
> The boy might as well have said that he was going to buy Dodger Stadium. He had arrived in Los Angeles that morning, with less than five dollars in his pocket and no change of clothes.
>
> I explained to him how long it would take for him to get a medical degree, and how much it would cost. With what tact I could summon, I pointed out that the whole idea was fantastic. I suggested alternatives which might be within his reach.
>
> He listened patiently and courteously. He was as respectful as he could be. But my words made no impression upon him. He wanted to be a doctor. He believed he could be a doctor, and a doctor he was going to be.
>
> With admiration bordering on astonishment, I watched that young man put himself through medical school, marry in the process, and graduate with honors. He is now a heart specialist in Los Angeles.

"Energy, invincible determination and then death or victory." Such is the law of success in every sphere of life, as is easily seen in the lives of successful men and women from every profession. Why should it not be so in the building of a righteous character? "And blessed are all they who do hunger and thirst after righteousness, for they shall be filled with the Holy Ghost." (3 Nephi 12:6, and Matt. 5:6.) This challenging principle becomes even more vivid when we study the conditions of Palestine and learn of the severe physical hunger and thirst that are experienced in that semi-desert land.

It is not uncommon for bath water to be drained off and used for irrigation purposes. So very scarce was water that Biblical writers frequently and effectively mention water in their figures of speech. I call your attention to only a few.

Perhaps the most poetic Old Testament writer, the psalmist, yearns, "As the hart panteth after the water brooks, so panteth my soul after thee, O God. My soul thirsteth for God, for the living God." (Psalm 42:1-2.)

Isaiah, searching for words to describe the happy future of Zion, tells his people, "For in the wilderness shall waters break out, and streams in the desert. And the parched ground shall become a pool, and the thirsty land springs of water." (Isaiah 35:6-7.)

When Jesus talks to the Samarian woman at the well, he tells her that if she will accept the water of life which he has to give, she will never thirst again. "Whosoever drinketh of the water that I shall give him shall never thirst; but the water that I shall give him shall be in him a well of water springing up into everlasting life." (John 4:14.)

John the Revelator even goes so far as to compare heaven to a place containing a crystal spring of water where one may drink as much as he pleases without charge. "I will give unto him that is athirst of the fountain of the water of life freely." (Rev. 21:6.) "And he shewed me a pure river of water of life, clear as crystal, proceeding out of the throne of God and of the Lamb." (Rev. 22:1.) "They shall hunger no more, neither thirst any more . . . for the Lamb . . . shall lead them unto living fountains of waters." (Rev. 7:16-17.)

Water is so hard to find in Palestine and the surrounding desert country that people almost go crazy from thirst. Food is so scarce that men and women are often compelled to live on a daily diet of no more than a few dates and a cup of milk, or even so little as a piece of hard bread. Under such conditions people naturally make the attainment of food and water the chief concern of their lives. Jesus contends that only when we are equally serious about attaining a righteous character, when we really hunger and thirst for righteousness, shall we be filled.

An outstanding teacher was once listening to his wife play a beautiful sonata on the piano. "I would give anything in the world to be able to play like that," he said.

"All right," she responded. "Let's see if you really mean that. You say that you would give anything in the world to be able to play as I have. I have given several hours a day almost every day for the last fifteen years. I have given up picnics and parties and many other kinds of entertainment in order to stay at my task. I have sacrificed the study of many interesting subjects; I have given and worked and worked and given until at times it seemed that I could not work another hour or sacrifice another thing. To play the piano as well as I do, would you be willing to give that much?"

"You've got me there," he admitted. "I thought I would give anything to be a great piano player. I realize now, that while I would give up a few things, I do not want this particular ability enough to sacrifice much time or many pleasures for its attainment."

"But you are a great teacher," she reminded him. "You have succeeded in your profession because you have done with your teaching what I have done with my music. You made it the first consideration of your life, sacrificing where others have not been willing to sacrifice, studying, working, and planning where others have not been willing to make the effort. You have sought first the kingdom of teaching, and this you have been able to achieve."

So Jesus would have us realize that in the building of a great balanced life, there is nothing mysterious or unusual about the above illustration. If we want to have mediocre spiritual houses, let us give a minimum of time and effort. If we want to build beautiful houses of life or to change the design of our present lives, if we wish to reach great heights in our upward climb toward nobleness or character, let us do away with all things and every

thought that hinders our progress. A mere public announcement of faith will little hasten our progress. Simply joining the Church and regularly attending all of the various meetings is no guarantee. Only when we put righteousness first in our thinking and without serious regret give up every conflicting desire shall we be able to reach the coveted goal, "because strait is the gate; and narrow is the way, which leadeth unto life, and few there be that find it." (Matt. 7:14, and 3 Nephi 14:14.)

The reason we have so many mediocre musicians is that there are only a few people who are willing to follow the narrow road that leads to great musicianship. We have so few great artists, lawyers, doctors, and teachers because only a few are willing to get rid of the excess baggage that prevents them from travelling the straight and narrow road. Herbert Hoover once warned, "We are in danger of developing a cult of the common man," which he went on to interpret to mean a cult of mediocrity. The great human advances have not been brought about by mediocre men and women; they have been achieved by distinctly uncommon people with vital sparks of leadership.

In Palestine a person who always looked at others with envy was referred to as having a "bad eye." One who stole was said to have a "long arm." Jesus, knowing that everyone would understand what he meant, told the people that it would be better for one to pluck out his right eye (envying others' wealth and honor) or cut off his hand (being unjust and dishonest) than to keep these bad habits and ruin the possibility of developing a fully rounded, well-balanced life. (Matt. 5:29.)

Does honesty always bring material reward? "Be good and you will be wealthy." I suspect that many of us believed that as children. However, some wealthy people are not honest, and some honest people have never had many wordly possessions. We miss the point of Jesus' teaching unless we realize that the reward of righteousness is something bigger, better, and more beautiful than material gain. Envy, dishonesty, and unfairness—all of these are excess baggage, and as such are not worth what it costs to carry them with us.

This principle is illustrated by an experience of a young friend of mine. Married, with two children, and living on a very small salary, he found it necessary to budget strictly. He and his wife spent only a few cents per meal for dessert for the whole family. He travelled all over town to find reasonable prices. Often when I asked him to go someplace, he replied, "Can't do it this week. I've used up my budget for gasoline."

One summer I found him a job doing some menial tasks that would be classified as unskilled labor. Since he was a college graduate and a high school teacher, I asked if he really enjoyed doing such work, if he found satisfaction in the bondage of such a restricted budget. He replied, "Of course, I don't enjoy it, but I do it because I'm anxious (hungry) to have a house of my own."

In conclusion, let me say, the house I mentioned at the beginning of the chapter was finally completed. It really is a beautiful structure. If I took you past it without telling you its history, I am quite certain that you would never guess. It had been black and unsightly, standing for months as nothing but the framework of a great purpose. Today it is a most attractive home. And it still talks to me, reminding me each time I see it that even adults, who have failed thus far, may still build beautiful and eternal lives.

Perhaps we spend too much time worrying about the mistakes of young people, forgetting that we as adults have the opportunity to continue building as the years go by. I suspect that the Lord was thinking of all ages and classes of people when he said, "Blessed are they which do hunger and thirst after righteousness: for they shall be filled." (Matt. 5:6, and 3 Nephi 12:6.) "Seek ye first the kingdom of God, and his righteousness; and all these things," whatever proves necessary for righteous people, "shall be added unto you." (Matt. 6:33, and 3 Nephi 13:33.)

REFLECTIONS ON THE VALUE
OF GOOD SPORTSMANSHIP

Sympathy is the safeguard of the human soul against selfishness.

—CARLISLE

It profits little to bury the hatchet and leave the handle sticking out.

—DWIGHT L. MOODY

Next to knowing when to seize an opportunity, the most important thing in life is to know when to forego an advantage.

—DISRAELI

I will speak ill of no man and speak all the good I know of everybody.

—BENJAMIN FRANKLIN

The man who lacks faith in other men loses his best chances to work and gradually undermines his own power and his own character.

—UNKNOWN

I have never knowingly planted a thorn in any human heart, but I have always endeavored to pluck a thorn and plant a rose wherever I thought a rose would grow.

—ABRAHAM LINCOLN

The true final examination in the thought of Jesus in any education for life has just one question, "How much does a person mean to you?" Have you learned really to be a good friend?

—HENRY C. KING

CHAPTER III

BE A GOOD SPORT

One of the Apocrypha books records an interesting story about the relationship of Jesus and another young boy. It tells us that one day as Jesus and Joseph were returning home, they met a young man who ran against Jesus and knocked him to the ground. Arising angrily, the boy Jesus said, "As thou hast thrown me down, so shalt thou fall, nor ever rise." (Lost Book of the Bible, p. 57.) In the same hour the boy fell down and died.

Now please do not think that I expect anyone to believe that story. I cannot; but I ask you to think how it would change our attitude and the attitude of the world toward Jesus if enough evidence could be produced to make us believe that story.

I cannot forget how my opinion of Michelangelo was changed when I first discovered in one of his paintings the evidence of a vindictive spirit. Standing recently in one of the long halls of the Vatican in Rome, I studied with a constantly increasing thrill one of the masterful pictures of the great artist, until one of the tour guides succeeded in dampening my appreciation with the following story.

> Do you see that section in the lower right hand corner of the picture? That represents hell. And do you see that man with the horns on his head and a serpent twisted about his loins? That is supposed to be Messer Biagio da Cesena, the pope's master of ceremonies, who once made light of some of Michelangelo's paintings, saying that his nude figures would be more suitable

for a place of debauchery than for the chapel of the pope. Resenting the criticism, Michelangelo proceeded to paint Messer Biagio da Cesena and place him in hell, a ghastly picture of a man with horns stuck into his head and a serpent winding about his body.

Messer da Cesena begged the pope to have his enemy punished, but the pope only replied, "Had the painter sent you to purgatory I would have used my best efforts to get you released, but I exercise no influence in hell." The figure still stands, and the picture is a constant reminder of Michelangelo's vengeful spirit.

Can you find evidence of such a spirit in the life of Jesus? He showed many other human characteristics. He became discouraged when the capital of his nation refused to heed his words, and he cried, "O Jerusalem, Jerusalem, thou that killest the prophets, and stonest them which are sent unto thee, how often would I have gathered thy children together, even as a hen gathereth her chickens under her wings, and ye would not!" (Matt. 23:37.) He became angry when his listeners found fault with him for healing on the Sabbath. (Mark 3:5.) When he was rebuked by his disciples for blessing little children, "he was much displeased." (Mark 10:14.) We may believe that he also disliked suffering, for he prayed to God in his last days of life that he might be saved from the agony of the cross if it were possible. Neither the Bible nor the Book of Mormon hides these facts from us. Yet in no place does either record hint that Jesus ever performed an unkind act. He was mocked; he was cursed; he was spit upon; he was severely beaten and cruelly nailed to the cross. Yet he showed not even the slightest sign of seeking revenge upon those who had mistreated him.

Few of us have met the persecution that he was compelled to endure. Still he was able to say with confidence, "Blessed are the merciful: for they shall obtain mercy." (Matt. 5:7, and 3 Nephi 12:7.) At close range, even at the moment of showing mercy, the principle may not always seem to work. But in the long run, he who practices it collects his reward.

Recognize your own need for growth, be humble—that is the first principle of successful living. Want righteousness so fervently that you make its attainment the first consideration of your life, sacrificing as much for it as you would sacrifice for food and water if you were dying of starvation and thirst—Christ's second principle of successful living. The third grows out of the other two: "be merciful," careful not to say anything about another that you would not want him to say about you. Similarly, be unwilling to do anything to another that you would not want him to do to you if your conditions of life were reversed.

A prominent professional man, well known for his sportsmanlike behavior, was asked by a newspaper reporter the reason for his generosity. "You have plenty of money," said the reporter. "You are popular, and you are on the way to the top. Why should you bother with others less fortunate than yourself?"

"It is true," replied the professional man. "I am on the way up, but the time may come when I shall be on the way down. I want to make plenty of friends while I am on the way up so that I shall have plenty of friends when I am on the way down."

Everyone who read this statement in the paper, I suppose, agreed that it expressed a good philosophy of life, and I imagine that the one who said it had no intention of making a religious confession. But long before this modern business executive gave expression to such a philosophy of life, Jesus gave the same principle:

"Blessed are the merciful: for they shall obtain mercy." (Matt. 5:7, and 3 Nephi 12:7.) "Give, and it shall be given unto you." (Luke 6:38.) "Judge not, that ye be not judged." (Matt. 7:1, and 3 Nephi 14:1.) "Therefore all things whatsoever you would that men should do to you, do ye even so to them: for this is the law and the prophets." (Matt. 7:12, and 3 Nephi 14:12.)

Would you like to build a mediocre life, a life that attracts few friends and knows little of the value of friendship and the finer qualities of character? Then be critical and hateful. Find fault with every person and every action you see. Be the fly in the ointment of everybody's joy; be a grouch; be heartless, cruel, and cold; and you

will accomplish what you desire. But, if on the other hand you want to be sure that others will be merciful to you when you need mercy, will be kind and loving toward you when you need sympathy, then forget your criticisms. Let bygones be bygones; stop being a grouch; judge not and you shall not be judged—be merciful and you shall obtain mercy.

Is this golden rule philosophy in the Bible? Is it in the Book of Mormon? Is it in other scriptures? Yes, but long before it was written in the scriptures it was found in the book of human experience. It is not a threat; it is a principle, but sooner or later intelligent people discover it to be inescapable.

In Palestine when a farmer wanted to sell his grain, he turned it over to a man who poured it into a measuring box, a box that looked something like the old peck measure. The grain was shaken and pressed down to make room for more grain. When the box was full and the grain heaped up into a peak, still more was poured upon it until the grain rolled down over the sides. So the people of Palestine understood full well what Jesus meant when he said, "Give, and it shall be given unto you; good measure, pressed down, and shaken together, and running over, shall men give unto your bosom. For with the same measure that ye mete withal it shall be measured to you again." (Luke 6:38.)

Madelyn S. Bridges puts it another way:

> Give love, and love to your life will flow
> And strengthen your inmost needs.
> Have faith and a score of hearts will show
> Their faith in your work and deeds.

> For life is the mirror of king and slave;
> 'Tis just what we are and do.
> Then give to the world the best you have,
> And the best will come back to you.

With what measure do ye mete?

Would you like to see how the principle works in actual life? Take a look at the negative side of King Saul. One day as he and his young companion, David, were returning from a battle, Saul became very jealous. While the crowds gave him the credit for killing thousands, they marveled at the tens of thousands that David had killed. With malice and jealousy eating at his heart, Saul made it one of the supreme purposes of his life to dispose of his youthful rival. Like a peeved child, he chased David from one part of the country to another, up and down the hills of Palestine, in and out of caves, back and forth from one road to another—always intent upon one thing: retaliation. You know the end of the story, how his soul shriveled up, and in sorrow and with courage spent, the once great king fell upon his own sword—a man who had not learned that *what you give, you get.*

Now, let us compare Saul with the leader of another nation. In the middle of a very cold winter William McKinley was riding about the country in a coach, campaigning for the presidency of the United States. When he discovered that there was another traveler on top of the coach, who was suffering because of the lack of an overcoat, Mr. McKinley invited him to ride inside the coach where he would be warm.

"But, Mr. McKinley," the man objected, "you don't know who I am. I am a reporter, and my newspaper has hired me to follow you about the country in order that I can report all the bad things I can discover about you and your campaign."

"All right," said Mr. McKinley, "keep on with the job if you want to; but if you wish to do it satisfactorily, you had better come in the coach and keep warm."

What a different story it would have been if King Saul could have had the spirit of William McKinley, and what a different story it would be in our lives if we were as willing as McKinley to follow the spirit of good sportsmanship, of sympathy, kindness, and mercy.

Booker T. Washington, one of the most successful leaders this country has ever known, said that the reason he would not fight with another person, the reason that he would not even say an evil thing against another, was because as a boy he had learned that the only way to keep another person in the ditch was to stay there with him. A man cannot condemn and hurt someone else without having an equal reaction on himself, at least from his own soul if not from the other individual also. "Blessed are the merciful: for they shall obtain mercy." (Luke 5:7, and 3 Nephi 12:7.) "Give, and it shall be given unto you." (Luke 6:38.)

Though it benefits us personally to be merciful unto others, we do not hear the full challenge of Jesus nor do we feel the expansive power of the soul until we go beyond the thought of personal reward. We honor good sportsmen wherever we find them—on the athletic field, in business, in politics, or in the social world. Unkindness and ingratitude have a cheap appearance and are below the level of a "squareshooter."

Nearly two thousand years ago Jesus laid emphasis upon the positive side of this spirit of fair play, admitting that the exercise of mercy will bring us personal reward. Jesus also said that we should be merciful because God had been so merciful to us. "He maketh his sun to rise on the evil and on the good, and sendeth rain on the just and on the unjust." (Matt. 5:45, and 3 Nephi 12:45.) As a Father who loves us even more than we love our children, he cannot help showering his blessings upon us. Is it not poor sportsmanship on our part to accept God's many gifts, the mercy he continually is showing us, and then refuse to be merciful ourselves toward others who make mistakes?

To illustrate his own feelings about such ungrateful behavior and the natural results that come from such attitudes, Jesus told the story of a certain king who "would take account of his servants. And when he had begun to reckon, one was brought unto him, which owed him ten thousand talents. But forasmuch as he had not to pay, his lord commanded him to be sold, and his wife, and children, and all that he had, and payment to be made. The servant therefore fell down, and worshipped him, saying, Lord, have patience with me, and I will pay thee all. Then the lord of that servant was moved with compassion, and loosed him, and forgave him the debt." (Matt. 18:23-27.)

The scripture does not say that the creditor suddenly fell in love with the poor fellow groveling at his feet. It merely tells us that the king had compassion upon the servant and forgave him his debt. Refusing to kick him when he was down, the king instead had mercy upon the man.

"Everybody talkin' about heaven, ain't goin' there." Yes, and all who talk about reaching the great height of love and sacrificial living who do not first achieve the plane of good sportsmanship may as well realize that they will never reach such heights. Mercy and courtesy are both phases of good sportsmanship, though neither of them is so complete and noble as love. Early in the building of a successful life we must include the principle of mercy. Whether we ever learn to love or not, we can still know the thrill that comes from being a good sport with God and our fellowman.

How little, mean, and shriveled is the soul of one who receives mercy from God, as we all have times without number, and who then stingily refuses to show mercy to his fellowman. In the story of the unmerciful servant Jesus held up a mirror that all of us might see the ugliness of such shriveled souls.

> But the same servant went out, and found one of his fellowservants, which owed him an hundred pence: and he laid hands on him, and took him by the throat, saying, Pay me that thou owest.
>
> And his fellowservant fell down at his feet, and besought him saying, Have patience with me, and I will pay thee all.
>
> And he would not: but went and cast him into prison, till he should pay the debt.
>
> So when his fellowservants saw what was done, they were very sorry, and came and told unto their lord all that was done.
>
> Then his lord, after that he had called him, said unto him, O thou wicked servant, I forgave thee all that debt, because thou

desiredst me: Shouldest not thou also have had compassion on thy fellowservant, even as I had pity on thee?

And his lord was wroth, and delivered him to the tormentors, till he should pay all that was due. (Matt. 18:28-34.)

Christ summarized the incident, "So likewise shall my heavenly Father do also unto you, if ye from your hearts forgive not every one his brother their trespasses." (Matt. 18:35.)

Whatever way we look at the matter, we find the unsportsmanlike person getting the worst of the deal. Being unmerciful, he receives little sympathy from his fellowmen; and by looking upon the world with a cold and selfish spirit, he not only misses many of life's greatest values but in the process his soul grows smaller. James Moffat indicates that the eye is the lamp of the body: so if your eye is generous, the whole of your body will be illumined; but if your eye is selfish, the whole of your body will be darkened. And if your very light turns dark, then what a darkness it is!

REFLECTIONS ON EFFECTIVE THINKING

The happiest person is the person who thinks the most interesting thoughts.

—Timothy Dwight

Nothing is so powerful as an idea when its hour has come.

—Victor Hugo

Two men looked out through the selfsame bars; one saw the mud, and the other saw the stars.

—Fredrick Langbridge

Great thoughts alone change men and women. By the great thoughts of Jesus men and women, for some two thousand years, have been changed from folly to the ways of wisdom, from baseness to unwholesomeness, from cruelty to mercifulness, from sin to righteousness.

—H.S. Johnson

Man must be arched and buttressed from within, else the temple wavers to the dust.

—Marcus Aurelius

Be not conformed to this world: but be ye transformed by the renewing of your mind, that ye may prove what is that good, and acceptable, and perfect, will of God.

—Romans 12:2

Whatsoever things are true, whatsoever things are honest, whatsoever things are just, whatsoever things are pure, whatsoever things are lovely, whatsoever things are of good report; if there be any virtue, and if there be any praise, think on these things.

—Philippians 4:8

CHAPTER IV

GET THE MOST
OUT OF YOUR THINKING

I suspect that when we read Jesus' principle for successful living, "Blessed are the pure in heart: for they shall see God" (Matt. 5:8, and 3 Nephi 13:8), most of us have a tendancy to think of it as a denunciation of vulgar thinking and obscene action. There is no doubt that Jesus placed much emphasis on this point. In one part of his Sermon on the Mount, he intimated that it was practically as bad to think obscene thoughts as it was to do vulgar things. "Ye have heard that it was said by them of old time, Thou shalt not commit adultery: But I say unto you, That whosoever looketh on a woman to lust after her hath committed adultery with her already in his heart." (Matt. 5:27-28, and 3 Nephi 12:27-28.)

But it is unfair to limit this principle to the absence of obscenity. The Savior was never very much concerned about the negative side of things. He seemed to feel that if one were active in a good cause, there would not be much chance of his falling into evil paths. The best way to stop doing wrong is to begin doing right. And the way to keep doing right, according to Jesus' philosophy, is to think always in the right way.

Such a principle is not confined to the field of religion. As one has well said, "The battle for kingly self-control is lost or won in the citadel of one's inmost soul."

Throughout the ages it has been understood in all fields of endeavor that a man becomes what he thinks.

A good example of this is the experience of Frank Wright. He was a switch engineer who smoked 22 cigars a day, had a voluminous vocabulary of profanity, and in general went his own way without much thought of consequences. Ministers and doctors both tried to guide him aright, but he paid no attention to their advice—until he finally got hold of the idea that if he could fill his mind with enough good thoughts, he would have little trouble and would greatly enjoy doing good.

Frank tried out the principle in his own life and it worked. He went to a reformatory in Michigan and was successful in getting six hundred inmates to apply the principle in their lives. The result was that out of three hundred and twenty released on parole the first year, only five of them found it necessary to return. According to the average, the number of returnees would have been one hundred and twelve.

The movement spread and became popular under the title "The Pathfinders of America." Many thousands of people have benefited from it and are yet broadcasting to the world the principle that as a man thinks, so is he. Fill the mind with bad thoughts, and they eventuate in weak lives. Keep the mind fresh, clean, and undisturbed by conflicting motives, and it will eventuate in constructive activity.

Not all thinking is helpful, because not all thinking is clear thinking. A beautiful stream of water, reflecting the grass, the flowers, the trees, and the clouds today, may become so muddied by a storm tomorrow that we are able to see in the water no sign of the beautiful reflection of the day before. So Jesus would have us know that only

As a man thinketh . . . so is he!

as we keep our minds unmuddied can we see plainly and correctly the truths of life.

Created in the image and likeness of our Heavenly Father, innocent children think quite clearly, perceiving life's truths more quickly sometimes than their elders would be willing to admit. But as the years pass by, prejudices creep into their thinking. Certain theological doctrines, political theories of an inherited party, social standards of our particular community or class, and even fears, personal hopes, and sorrow—all tend to muddy the stream of our mental processes. The result is that we often find it difficult to reason with any degree of clarity.

One day when Peter and John were going up to the temple, they came upon a poor beggar who had been lame since birth. When the man asked for alms, Peter "took him by the right hand, and lifted him up: and immediately his feet and ankle bones received strength." (Acts 3:7.)

The act of healing and Peter's subsequent speech aroused the anger of the Sadducees, who imprisoned Peter and John. The two were finally released for diplomatic reasons. But hearing later that Peter and John were still preaching, the Sadducees threw them once more into jail and recommended that they be put to death.

The apostles had done nothing worthy of such punishment. They had killed no one. They had stolen no money. They had not caused anyone serious trouble. The Sadducees had simply allowed themselves to do some muddy thinking. They did not believe in the resurrection, and here were two men who dared to stand in their presence and preach enthusiastically a doctrine that was diametrically opposed to their beliefs. Peter's words were the storm that muddied the stream, stirring up emotions and prejudices that destroyed all possibility of logical reasoning.

How often do we see theological and political dogmatism doing the same thing today! Let a conservative start to talk before a group of liberals, and, more often than not, his doctrines have little chance of being considered. When a liberal pleads his cause before a group of conservatives, he will usually find himself at the same disadvantage.

A humorous illustration of this was brought to my attention a few years ago. One evening on a university campus a Mr. _____ spoke on a particular political and economic point of view. Some very prejudiced members of a campus organization broadcasted their presence by sitting near the front. When asked later how they had liked the speech, the young men said they considered it a very poor talk. Pressed for a more specific statement, they were compelled to admit that they had not listened; and when questioned as to the reason for such discourtesy, they replied, "Because we cannot accept the theology of Professor _____." The irony was that the speaker was not Professor _____, but a man who lived in the same town with these "good brethren," and who accepted the same theological view to which they themselves subscribed.

In the before-cited account from the Book of Acts, there was at least one man who knew how, and was willing, to think clearly. Gamaliel told the rest of the court members that it would be not only unfair but also unwise to mete harsh punishment to Peter and John. Others had arisen from time to time who had drawn quite a following after them, but their popularity had not been long lived. "And now I say unto you, Refrain from these men, and let them alone: for if this counsel or this work be of men, it will come to nought: But if it be of God, ye cannot overthrow it; lest haply ye be found even to fight against God. And to him they agreed: and when they had called the apostles, and beaten them, they commanded that they should not speak in the name of Jesus, and let them go." (Acts 5:38-40.)

As soon as Gamaliel brought God into the picture, the stream of the court members' thinking cleared, and they were able to see things in a much better light. Jesus had said, "Blessed are the pure in heart: for they shall see God." (Matt. 5:8, and 3 Nephi 12:8.) Perhaps we are justified in turning the statement around and reasoning: Blessed are they who, like Gamaliel, see God, for they shall do pure, unadulterated, unmuddied thinking.

Another thing that confuses our minds and makes it difficult to think clearly is selfish desires. I suggest the following true story to illustrate both sides of the principle.

When a manager of a supermarket, I was approached by a friend who wanted me to help him obtain a position with another firm. Feeling that he was not quite the person for the organization, I told him so very frankly. Of course, he disagreed with me and proceeded to give what he considered to be sufficient evidence to prove his point. On another occasion he asked for a change of opinion, and when I found it necessary to reiterate my earlier statement, he became angry and filled the air with descriptive adjectives.

That was the first act in our little drama. The second occurred when I went to speak before a group of community leaders, among whom he was a leading figure. I wondered if he would listen to anything that I had to say. By his own discourtesy, would he cause others in the audience to think my talk of no value? I confess I went to the gathering with considerable misgivings, only to find that my friend was one of my best and most sympathetic listeners. After the meeting he came to me in the same friendly way that he had come once before, showing not the slightest sign that there had been any disagreement between us.

What was the reason for the Dr. Jekyll-Mr. Hyde behavior? In our earlier meetings, self-interest had been uppermost in my friend's mind and had so muddied his thinking that he had found it practically impossible to reason clearly. Between our two meetings, he had asked himself the questions, "What would the Lord prefer to have in this instance? What would be *his* solution to this problem?" and immediately the emotional storm had passed by. The stream of his thinking was clear; and he was able to see, if not my viewpoint, at least my right to think as I pleased.

"Blessed are the pure in heart: for they shall see God." And, blessed are they who see the Lord in every situation, for they shall do pure thinking—they shall think clearly and logically. Instead of seeking political positions for the honor and the salary attached to them, men will think of these jobs as opportunities for the discovery and expression of justice and truth.

In the business and professional world, those who think clearly will use money for the making of men instead of using men to make money. With minds unclouded by the thought of material gain and unruffled by the urge of selfish ambition, employers will be able to see what many have learned to understand: that "man shall not live by bread alone" (Matt. 4:4), that "a man's life consisteth not in the abundance of the things which he possesseth" (Luke 12:15), and that "he that heareth my word, and believeth on him that sent me, hath everlasting life." (John 5:24.)

Jesus does not say that a clear-thinking, clean person must wait until the next life to reap his reward. Here and now, in the midst of mortality, such a person can have an abundant life. And such a life is not made up of bank accounts, political offices, or the praise of the rabble. These may give a passing satisfaction, but *life*—this eternal value which Jesus speaks of as being possible here and now as well as in the eternities—is something more than bread and commodities which pass with the days.

Eternal life, whether in the life to come or here in this world, is made up of eternal elements: love which cannot die, friendships and loyalty which even the threat of death cannot destroy, a name whose price is above that of rubies, a soul in which the seed of the kingdom of God grows continually larger and larger. Minds that are confused and adulterated by an over-abundance of selfish desire are not capable of seeing the worth of such values.

Unless we are careful, suffering and sorrow may also muddy our thinking. Witness the following case: Upon the death of a prominent man, his widow, who had been a woman of great faith and sterling character, almost lost her sense of values. She quit going to church. She stopped speaking to many of her friends. One day when I called on her, she rejoiced because she had a cold, saying that she hoped it would become sufficiently severe to take her from this life. When I scolded her gently for such an attitude, she said, "Why should I live? There is nothing left to live for." You see, she was not thinking clearly; her mind was muddied because of her great sorrow at her husband's death.

She had nothing to live for? Think how it would have increased her faith if she had gone back to her friends saying, "My companion and I are separated for a short time, but I know that God lives, and I still know the gospel to be true." Nothing to live for! Yet there were scores of people who loved her, who wanted to help and who needed her help. There were lonely folks who would have risen up in this life and in the next to call her blessed, if she had been willing to visit them and bring them the joy of her friendship. There were church classes to be taught by well-trained leaders like herself. There were young people who needed the guidance of intelligent, sympathetic adults. But she saw none of these possibilities. Her sorrow had diluted her sense of reason.

Leaving her darkened home, I went to call at another home, where death had come only a few days before. As I talked to the parents about the loss of their teenage son, I saw tears but I sensed no evil rebound to their unhappy situation. They still believed in God and in the beauty of his creations. They talked openly and proudly about the work that their son had done in the church; as a family they wanted to continue what he had begun so well. They loved their son's friends and associates and felt a keen responsibility toward them, and toward the world in general. In fact, the attitude of the entire family was so beautiful and so hopeful that I could not keep from speaking of it in their presence.

The mother and father replied, "Of course, we shall greatly miss our son. He was so devoted to all of us. But when we stop to think calmly about the whole matter, we remember that it was our Father and his Son who made the universe. It was God who created man. And through His divine plan man is given the opportunity to continue his work and the joy of life beyond the veil. So long as we see and know God and his purposes, we are content."

There is a difference, isn't there, between facing calamity with a mind that sorrow prohibits from doing its best thinking and meeting the same difficulty with a mental process that has been purified by the knowledge of the existence of a loving Father.

The president of one of our great universities once wrote, "You can solve all the problems of the world if you think on them long enough." But if that were true, then why the great international and inter-class difficulties that face us today? Have the people of any nation ever thought harder than those of the United States during the last few decades? Yet with every thought there has come another pile of atom bombs for potential destruction.

Could a people think more desperately than the Vietnamese have during the last few years? Yet with their thinking, war has become more deadly and hatred more intense. Egypt and Israel have been doing some pretty hard thinking, and the Chinese and Russians have done their share. Yet, wars continue to rage. Hatreds grow more and more inflamed not only between nations, but also between capitalists and laborers, between conservatives and progressives in politics, between fundamentalists and modernists in religion, and between light and dark colors among races of men. Diluted knowledge, prejudice and selfish desires, and the loss of faith in God had muddied our thinking and kept us from seeing and properly evaluating situations and facts.

It is not thinking, but *purified* thinking that finds correct solutions to individual, group, national, and international problems. Unmuddied thinking raises individuals from the level of savages into the sphere of sons and daughters of an Eternal Father.

"Blessed are the pure in heart: for they shall see God." (Matt. 5:8, and 3 Nephi 12:8.) Blessed are they who see God, for they shall do pure thinking. Read it either way, and you get the same results—a principle that cannot be evaded, the observance of which will build and expand the soul of every individual and every nation that is willing to follow where it leads.

REFLECTIONS ON MAKING PEACE
WITHOUT THE USE OF FORCE

Peace cannot be kept by force. It can only be achieved by understanding.
                                        —ALBERT EINSTEIN

The crest and crowning of all good, life's final star, is brotherhood.
                                        —EDWIN MARKHAM

You cannot kill a wrong idea except with a right idea.
                                        —MAUDE ROYDEN

Perfect love casteth out fear.   —I JOHN 4:18

Fences are inadequate protection against jungles — the ultimate and basic protection against the jungle is the cultivation of gardening. And likewise, the ultimate and basic protection against the social jungle is the cultivation of character.
                                        —RALPH W. SOCKMAN

CHAPTER V

MAKE PEACE WITHOUT THE USE OF FORCE

"Blessed are the peacemakers: for they shall be called the children of God." (Matt. 5:9, and 3 Nephi 12:9.) This is one of Jesus' great principles of successful living. But before we note the application of this principle to our modern day, I would like to tell you, for the purpose of illustration, about two different bodies of water about which I have had a little experience.

One was on a little hill in the countryside in the state of Arkansas. On a day when I had nothing of importance to do — I was only a youngster at the time — I threw my fishing pole over my shoulder and, in company with several friends, wandered across the fields to a quiet little pond. It was a beautiful spot, a peaceful place, with hardly a ripple on the surface of the water and only an occasional cawing of a crow to remind one of the life of the world.

We sat down, put some worms on our hooks, threw them into the water, leaned back, and just waited: one hour, two hours, three hours, four hours — without catching a single fish and not so much as a single nibble on our hooks. Later we learned from those who knew the place better than we that it was a new pond and one in which, to their knowledge, there had never been any fish of any kind. A peaceful spot? Yes, beautiful, restful, peaceful, but it was to a sportsman a negative peace.

On another day I stood by the shore of a tumultuous river which hissed and roared and threw itself against its banks like some great monster that had been recently set free from captivity — the last thing in the world that one would think of as being peaceful. Yet I was told that because of this river's very turbulent spirit and the power with which it threw itself over the falls onto the rocks beneath, it was able to turn the wheels of factories which made suitable clothing for men, women, and children, and produced electricity which brought light and power to homes and industries along its course. Peaceful? No, but surely none would deny that it was a *maker* of peace.

Now, I suggest to you that these two bodies of water represent quite vividly the two pictures of peace that are described in the scriptures. In the Old Testament, it was a green pasture and a stream of still water to which a faithful shepherd had led his sheep. It was a table prepared for one in the presence of his enemies, soothing oil with which to rub the wounded head, a cup of cool, sparkling water in a dry and thirsty land, a safe passage through the valley of the shadow of death, and quiet restfulness in the house of the Lord forever. (Psalms 23.)

One cannot criticize such a picture any more than he could destroy the blessed peace of the quiet country pond. But restful and comforting as it is for certain moments in our lives, if we would live abundantly, we will not fail to see the turbulent activities of One who brought peace to others and found peace for himself — not in withdrawing from but in throwing himself against the sins, follies, weaknesses and frivolities of human-kind.

The protection of childhood and womanhood, the new light of love in our homes, the powers of gospel ideals which through the years, through the centuries, have been growing through industry and government,

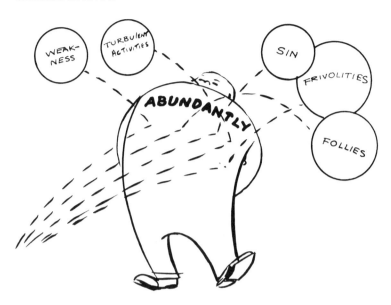

have come to the world through the Savior's radiant sacrificing life and the loyalty that he demonstrated in his death. Is it any wonder, therefore, that when he called men and women to follow as his disciples he said to them, "Blessed are the peacemakers"? (Matt. 5:9, and 3 Nephi 12:9.) He did not say, "Blessed are those who because of great wealth have no worries about material necessities." He did not talk about the peace of those who are physically so strong that they have no worry about discouraging illness. He was not describing the joy of those who easily gain social distinction and political power. Rather, did he say, "Blessed are the peace-*makers*," those who, regardless of how much or how little they may have in material or mental powers, are willing to throw themselves against the sins and frailties and the devastating riots of humanity, destroying evil and bringing in its stead a new kind of peace — one whch surpasses the understanding of who are merely quiet.

The challenge is how to become successful peace-

makers. Several methods have been tried. The early
Christian church endeavored to bring peace to its members by building walls about them and by protecting
them in every way that they could from the things in life
that caused unrest. Even at the time of their baptism,
candidates were required to "renounce the devil and all
his works." And by the "works of the devil," they referred among other things to many kinds of social amuse-
ment. The farther one could get away from the world

Is solitude the answer for peace?

the better. Those who lived alone in caves or even on
the tops of high poles where they would not be affected
by the temptations of the world were thought to have the
best chance of developing saintly characters. Witness

the case of Simeon Stylites, born in 338 A.D., who spent several months one summer buried to his neck in the garden and later lived for thirty years on the top of a pillar sixty feet high. When he died, his body was embalmed and carried in magnificent procession to Antioch where it was placed in one of Constantine's churches.

Later during the same period of the apostasy, the church attempted to protect its people by letting a few of the priests do the thinking for the rest of the members. A good case to see how seriously the church carried out this plan is here cited: I remember as an undergraduate student hearing one of my distinguished professors in religion tell of an early book in which the author con-

tended that the Bible should be translated so that women and children could understand it. The church had refused to allow this. And on the margin of this book, a loyal churchman had written a statement declaring that any author was a heretic who would advise allowing women and children to read the Bible. He wrote into the margin of this book the same statement when he found the author contending that workmen and slaves should have the right and ability to read the Bible.

But you cannot stop all men from thinking, no matter how you protect them. And when you have thinking, you have disturbances. Certainly we can be convinced today that this method of making peace — protecting men and women from temptation and from the difficulty of facing the truth — can never bring the kind of peace that the Savior had in mind.

A second method of bringing peace is that of the militarist who evidently is sincere in the belief that if we can build big enough armies and navies to scare the rest of the world, we shall no longer have any international difficulties. "Have war to end war," is their slogan. But it is rather difficult to accept this philosophy in the face of continuous preparation of most of the nations to combat the preparation of their opponents.

Is a big stick the answer?

Christ promised that we would get from others if we would first give to others. Give love and we get love; give hatred and we get hatred in return. Try to build bigger armies and navies than other nations, and other nations will try to build armies and navies bigger than ours. Our past world wars did not build friendships; they invited enmity. They did not make the world safe for democracy or for any other decent form of government. We are still at swords' points throughout the world. The more we prepare for war, the more we want to fight, and the more we fight the harder the other fellow fights back in return. It is no longer a theory. Experience proves the fallacy of the argument that peace can be made by war.

The third method is that suggested by the general principle of the Lord. Ernest Ligon in his book, *The Psychology of Christian Personality,* tells us that there are just three things that cause war. Protect mankind as much as you can, build the largest armies and navies possible, make the most wonderful peace treaties known to man, but you will still have war as long as you have three certain elements in the world.

What are they? Fear, anger, and greed (lust). Ligon says such terms as "national prosperity and high standards of living which may have admirable ideals are often the dignified means of lust for the satisfaction of primitive appetites. Likewise, fears may be disguised under the name national security, self-preservation, race purity; and patriotism is often nothing more than a form of anger. Wars are a result of these same three personal conflicts. War would be impossible between nations composed dominantly of Christian personalities. It is the presence of those three elements which makes propaganda effective."

The real challenge is how to get rid of these three things in society. How can that be done? Jesus tells us

What are three certain elements that destroy peace?

the story of a man who had a demon. The demon left
him and wandered about in waterless places. But in
time it came back and, finding the house swept clean and
nothing in it, it entered therein with seven more demons
to keep it company. Jesus said that the condition of the
man was then worse than it had been before. (Matt. 12:
43-45.)

We cannot get rid of weakness in character until we

put something stronger in its place. We cannot be safe from the demonic work of fear, anger, and greed merely by driving these demons out of society. The sensible thing and the only safe thing to do is to put something more powerful in the place of these demons. The mind and the soul cannot remain a vacuum. When one thing is driven out, something must be put in its place or else it will return.

What shall we say about fear and anger toward others? Are such demons likely to enter the mental and spiritual house where there is fully developed appreciation? Some years ago while we were residing in California my small daughter once asked for the privilege of buying some articles in a neighborhod store. When I asked in return where she expected to go, she replied, "Well, I know one thing, I am not going to buy anything from that old Jew around the corner." And when I sought the reason for her attitude, she said, "Mary's mother says that Jews are all bad. They all cheat. They will skin you out of your last dollar."

When Jesus found the people holding similar attitudes toward the Samaritans he did not waste time with argument but placed in their minds the picture of one of the best Samaritans — a good man, a kind man, a thoughtful, helpful Samaritan — and then left it there to do its work. Would it not help us to feel more kindly toward our enemies, whoever they might be, if we could see a picture of some of their greater souls?

I remember my father-in-law once saying to a congregation of prospective Jewish rabbis, "We can have no civil marriages without your Mendelssohn, no theory of philosophy without your Spinoza, no anthology of verse without your Heine. Our Victorina Age lacks its chief ornament without Disraeli. And today we have your

Brandeif in jurisprudence, your Strauss and Rosenwald in philanthropy, your Flexner and Einstein in science." It might help to remember also that Amos, Hosea, Micah, Isaiah, Jeremiah, and Ezekiel were all Jews; the apostle Paul was a Jew, and even Jesus was a member of that race in his bodily form.

One day I was in company with a high school baseball team that was scheduled to play before a large group of Oriental students. One of the members of the team said, "Why do we have to play those Chinks?" "Chinks" are they, who had a well-established civilization before our ancestors came out of the jungle? "Chinks" are they, who gave to the world the mariner's compass, the printing press, paper, and other valuable inventions? "Chinks" are they who produce Confucius, one of the great statesmen of all time? "Chinks" are they, who brought into the world 300 years before the birth of Christ the great philosopher Moti, who taught even in those early days that love is the final solution to all worldly problems.

"But we can't say anything good about the Russians or the North Vietnamese." Should those who live in glass houses throw stones? A former teacher of mine used to cite the parable of three robbers. One did his stealing at 10 p.m., the other at 12 midnight, and the third at 2 a.m. The last man going to the two places where the others had been and finding nothing left, returned to the home where the other two robbers had collected their loot. In the meantime they had been converted, and when they saw him coming they began to preach to him. He repented also, but seeing the great pile of things which they had stolen, he remonstrated — and a war began.

Does this not represent quite well the international thievery and warfare? Without condoning the ruthlessness of the communistic Chinese and the Russian leaders in recent years, may we not properly ask what others would do if they were living under similar circumstances and bound by their ignorance? The Japanese and German armies did some terribly things during World War II. And we find that Russia, China, North Vietnam, and maybe others are following similar courses today. But then, who among the nations that might seek to block such efforts (necessary, as this might be) would come with clean hands?

It wouldn't be Britain, with her record in the Opium War. It couldn't be France with her record toward colonial possessions and occupied territories. Not Belgium, surely, with her reeking record in the Congo. Not Spain, nor Germany, which grabbed off one of the fattest segments of Africa's heart when the grabbing was good; nor Japan, who a few years ago had her teeth set in China's torn flanks. Nor yet the United States, with long centuries behind her of infamous mistreatment of our own Indians. Out of all history, you will find but one world conqueror who came with clean hands — and those were the hands of the Master, the Savior of the world.

And what shall we say about greed and lust? If they are partly the cause of animosity and strife between individuals and nations, disposing of them may do more good than the making of laws against crimes and the signing of peace treaties between nations. What shall we put in the place of greed and lust and how may the transfer be made in our lives and in the lives of the younger generation?

In reply to these questions, I suspect Jesus would place before us again and advise us to keep constantly in mind, the fact that life is something much bigger than material values. We quote his statement, ". . . life consisteth not in the abundance of . . . things," (Luke 12:15) then we

Only one world conqueror came with clean hands.

proceed to spend about nine-tenths of our time helping
and working for things.

The reason we do not get rid of greed in our lives is
that we do not believe Christ's statement strong enough
to give it a controlling place in our minds. Let us once
accept with all our hearts his philosophy of higher values
and let us focus our attention completely upon the attainment of those values for ourselves and for our fellowmen,
and there will not be any space left for lust and greed.

When parents have adhered faithfully to such a policy
in their own lives, they will have done much to build an

In dad's shadow.

appreciation of such values in the lives of their children. But where the father laughs at the smartness of the artful dodge in politics, where the mother sighs after the tinsel and toys that she knows have been bought with corrupt cash, where the conversation at the meal table steadily, though often unconsciously, lifts and lauds those who are out after the "real things," the eager ears about the board drink it in and childish hearts resolve what they will do when they have a chance. Where no voice speaks for high things, where no tide of indignation against wrong sweeps into language, where the children never feel that the parents have great moral and spiritual convictions — where there is no vision, the people perish.

If we would be successful between nations and individuals, and between the wearing spirits within ourselves, we must help to build up within our own minds and in the thinking of the younger generation the philosophy of the Savior. He had such confidence in his fellowmen that he could let them kill him and in the process still believe that they would someday lift his name to heaven in praise. So great was his love for mankind that he could always be patient, long-suffering, and sympathetic with those of every race and class. His sense of proper evaluation enabled him, in the face of material temptation, to find meat to eat that others know not of and to find his joy in the smile of a little babe and the thankful response of a beggar whom he had helped. Thus should we forget what we have done for others and always remember what others have done for us.

Whatever else we may do as individuals or nations, we shall never have peace in any lasting form until we have driven out the devils of anger, fear, and greed. And we shall never succeed in keeping these demonic urges out of our minds until we have replaced them with his love and his faith and his appreciation of the abundant life, as contained in the gospel of Jesus Christ.

REFLECTIONS ON THANK GOD FOR YOUR COMPETITORS

Let us pray not for a light burden, but a strong back.
—Theodore Roosevelt

It is by affliction chiefly that the heart of man is purified and that the thoughts are fixed on a better state."
—Samuel Johnson

He hath seen but half the universe who never has been shown the house of pain.
—Ralph Waldo Emerson

That which is perfected by a furnace — heat withstands the flame.
—Anon.

I have a horror of that sort of softness which is apt to grow over one like moss if one is not occasionally knocked about a little!"
—Maude Royden

It is the resistance that puts us on our mettle; it is the conquest of the reluctant stuff that educates the worker. I wish you enough difficuly to keep you well and make you strong and skillful."
—Henry Van Dyke

I am a cripple. I cannot realize it. Feel as if I could jump up and race you to the letter box this very minute. I am perfectly well — only I'm not. Nevertheless, a handicap may be a pathway to publicity . . . an incentive to ingenuity . . . a stimulus to introspection . . . a revealer of human sympathy . . . a textual illuminant . . . the exegesis of certain parts of the holy book can never be fully comprehended by one who has never passed through the veil of pain and privation."
—Arthur Churchman

CHAPTER VI

THANK GOD FOR YOUR COMPETITORS

A young father and mother had lost another child. I say "another" because, although these parents were still in their thirties, they had been blessed with four beautiful children, only to see three of them, one after another, pass out of this life into the other world.

Talking with them after the death of their last child, I tried my best to say a word that would bring them some comfort. I spoke of my warm friendship for them, of the great faith that they had shown in their Heavenly Father, of the beautiful spirit they exemplified — but I was not allowed to finish. The husband was saying in a particularly calm voice: "I thank you for your deep interest in our home. But you need not worry about us. We have gone through a terrible ordeal, but we are all right now. You see, we still have our faith in the gospel of Jesus Christ and in the restored Church, and we have each other."

I am thankful that they did not blame God for the loss of their children. I do not believe many people could worship a divine being who would step into a home and take from parents the most precious possession of their lives. What the young couple had intimated was that God our Heavenly Father, instead of being against them, was for them; not killing them, but through his Son giving them strength, and helping them to win a victory over the destructive power of calamity.

Why must the righteous suffer? No one knows all the answers, and the scriptures tell us but very little in attempting to find answers to that particular question. Moses, in recording the third chapter of Genesis, indicated that some types of hardship do come from sin. Why must women bring children into life through pain? It is because the first woman transgressed against a divine commandment that she might fulfill her destiny as a woman—to become a mother, even by mortal physical pain. (Gen. 3:13-16.) Why must man work from morning until night, day after day and year after year? It is because our father Adam disobeyed. (Gen. 3:17-19.) And why must man die? It is because he ate of the tree of the forbidden fruit. "And the Lord God said, 'Behold, the man is become as one of us, to know good and evil: And now, lest he put forth his hand, and take also the tree of life, and eat, and live forever; therefore the Lord God sent him forth from the Garden of Eden, to till the ground from whence he was taken." (Gen. 3:22-23.)

The Book of Ecclesiastes was very probably put in the Bible not for the sake of its positive teaching, but in order to show the extremes to which one would go who accepted a materialistic philosophy of life. The author contends that he has tried to find pleasure in numerous ways, and still he is not satisfied.

"I have seen all the works that are done under the sun; and, behold, all is vanity and a striving after wind. . . . I have gotten great wisdom . . . I applied my heart to know wisdom and to know madness and folly . . . I said in my heart, Come now, I will try thee with mirth . . . with wine . . . I made me great works; I builded me houses; I planted me vinyeards; I made me gardens and parks, and I planted trees in them of all kinds of fruit; I made me pools of water . . . I had great possessions of herds and flocks . . . I gathered me also silver and gold, and the treasure such as kings and the providences have

as their own; I got me men-singers and women-singers
... So I was great, and increased more than all that were
before me in Jerusalem . . . and behold, all was vanity
and a striving after wind, and there was no profit under
the sun." (Ecc. 1:14 to 2:11, Masoretic Text.)

According to the writer of Ecclesiasties, even being
good does not assure one of ultimate peace. Good and
bad alike are blessed and cursed. "All go unto one place;
all are of the dust, and all turn to dust again." (Ecc.
3:20.) ". . . There is a righteous man that perisheth in
his righteousness, and there is a wicked man that pro-
longeth his life in evil-doing. Be not righteous overmuch;
neither make thyself overwise. . . . Be not overmuch
wicked, neither be thou foolish . . ." (Ecc. 7:15-17, Masoretic Text.)

In the 60th chapter of the Book of Alma is recorded
General Moroni's second epistle to Pahoran. A question
concerning why the righteous perish is raised and beau-
tifully answered. "Do ye suppose that, because so many of
your brethren have been killed it is becaue of their wick-
edness? I say unto you, if ye have supposed this ye have
supposed in vain; for I say unto you, there are many who
have fallen by the sword; and behold it is to your con-
demnation; for the Lord suffereth the righteous to be
slain that his jusice and judgment may come upon the
wicked; therefore ye need not suppose that the righteous
are lost because they are slain; but behold, they do enter
into the rest of the Lord their God." (Alma 60:12-13.)

The author of the Book of Job tells us that not all
punishment comes from sin. Having lost his animals, his
servants, and his children, and having been tormented
with painful boils, Job is told by his friend that his suffering is the result of sin. He denies it. He says that he
has not sinned and that if he only had a chance, he would
tell God all about it.

Job's friends continue to argue with him. He tries his best to find an answer to the question, Why do the righteous suffer? but although much time passes and his suffering continues, he is unable to find the exact answers. A solution to the problem, which is better than an answer to his question, comes in a way that he has not expected. Why do the righteous suffer? He does not know exactly. But he wisely concludes that as long as he believes in the existence of a just God who knows and is concerned about him, he does not need to know all of the answers.

Elder Harold B. Lee has observed that living the gospel of Jesus Christ is no guarantee that adversity will not come into one's life. But living the gospel does give us the strength and faith and power to rise above that adversity and look beyond the present-day trouble to a brighter day.

Adversity, in one form or another, is the universal experience of man. It is the common lot of all men

to experience misfortune, suffering, sickness, or other adversities. It is the basic consequence of the law of free agency. Wherever there is a choice, there is a result. Some choices bring happiness and pleasure, others, affliction and sadness. Henry Ward Beecher said, "Affliction comes to all of us, not to make us sad, but sober; not to make us sorry, but to make us wise; not to make us despondent, but by its darkness to refresh us as the night refreshes the day; not to impoverish but to enrich us." It is only in the process of overcoming affliction and adversity that we become more like God.

Our children often wonder why we make them work when they would prefer to go swimming; why we compel them to study when they would much rather watch television; why we punish them sometimes when we still claim to love them better than anyone else. And it is only when they grow older and become parents themselves that they can fully understand. Would it not be well for us as children of the Creator to try to believe the same thing about him, and about his willingness, not perhaps to send trouble but to allow us to suffer at times when trouble comes?

Why not fun all day?

We take our next step in learning to conquer trouble when we turn to the teachings of Jesus. Does he always tell us why we suffer? No. But he gives us two important suggestions concerning the problem. He tells us that there is one thing upon which we can depend — if we do anything worthwhile, we are going to be persecuted.

It recalls to my mind the statement of an old man about his experience and the experience of other boys in the "old swimming hole." "When one of the fellows

Why should the "good guys" get hit?

stuck his head above the water, somebody always threw mud in his face." I remember a very successful teacher saying to me one time, "Paul, whenever I go into a community or to a new area and find no one willing to throw rocks at me, I feel that I am not striking very hard at evil. The more people criticize, the more I know that I am doing something worthwhile."

So the Savior said to his apostles: ". . . They will deliver you up to the councils, and they will scourge you in their synagogues; and ye shall be brought before governors and kings for my sake. . . . But when they deliver you up, take no thought how or what ye shall speak: for it shall be given you in that same hour what ye shall speak. . . . And ye shall be hated of all men for my name's sake: but he that endureth to the end shall be saved." (Matt. 10:17-22.)

As a general thing, evil will not bother us as long as we let it alone; but when we start to dislodge it, it fights back with venom. One thing of which we can be tolerably certain: if we are not being persecuted by wicked people, we are not doing much that is worthwhile in the building of the kingdom.

> You have no enemies, you say?
> Alas, my friend, the boast is poor!
> He who has mingled in the fray
> Of duty that the brave endure
> Must have made foes. If you have none,
> Small is the work that you have done.
> You have hit no traitor on the hip,
> You have dashed no cup from purged lip,
> You have never turned a wrong to right,
> You have been a coward in the fight.
>
> —COUNT VON ANERSPERG

In the second place, Jesus tells us that instead of worrying about persecution we ought to rejoice in the privilege of facing it. "Blessed are they which are persecuted for righteousness' sake. . . . Blessed are ye, when men shall revile you, and persecute you, and shall say all manner of evil against you falsely, for my sake. Rejoice, and be exceedingly glad: for great in your reward in heaven: for so persecuted they the prophets which were before you." (Matt. 5:10-12, and 3 Nephi 12:10-12.)

When a man walks along on a level surface, he breathes a certain amount of oxygen. But when he climbs a hill the percentage of oxygen that he takes into his lungs is very much increased. So athletes in the development of strong physical bodies often climb hills and hike over mountains and do a great deal of running in high altitudes whenever they have the chance. Children learn mathematics not merely by reading books, but by solving innumerable problems. It is hard work to think; but if we would develop the mind, we must think through different problems. Life grows as we face difficulty and conquer. No amount of alibis will take the place of such mental and spiritual exercise.

May I suggest that the way to deal with trouble is not just to bear it strongly, but to use it. Let us think of it as a problem to solve, let us use it as a hill to climb. It may seem difficult, it may be hard to endure. It is sometimes hard to climb a hill or to solve a problem; but what would life be like if we never climbed any physical hills and never solved any mental and spiritual problems? No wonder the Savior told us to rejoice and be exceedingly glad in the presence of persecution!

I remember one day several years ago listening to a series of lectures upon the prophets of the Old Testament. At one point the instructor was laying particular emphasis upon their great heroism in the face of evil persecution, when a young student asked with considerable anxiety: "Do you think I will ever be required to undergo such persecution? I don't believe I could possibly bear it." The thing she did not realize was that the prophets were made strong and courageous and a great deal better by their persecution. (Consider for a moment the persecution and the plight of the pioneers.)

Think, for instance, how backward Jeremiah was when he was first called to be a prophet of God, "Ah, Lord God!" he said, "behold, I cannot speak; for I am a child." But Jehovah said: ". . . Behold, I have made thee this day a fortified city and an iron pillar, and brazen walls, against the whole land. . . ." (Jer. 1:6, 18, Masoretic Text.) And then Jehovah proceeded to throw him out into the midst of trouble. Men mocked him, they threw him into a dungeon, they threatened to kill him, and they even refused to allow him to retire in his own hometown. But through this very persecution, he became a powerful leader for God. The walls that Jehovah had built about him were really molded out of that very persecution that men threw against him.

Prophets and other great men throughout all the ages have developed strong spiritual muscles through the climbing of mountainous roads of suffering and persecution. The steeper the incline, the more oxygen we breathe, the more exercise we gain.

It is a universal rule which applies in the physical, the mental, and the spiritual fields of experience. No one worries about it in athletics. The higher the obstacle we have to jump and the greater the competition we are compelled to meet, the more thrill we get out of the game and the better the results we obtain. We do not blame God or the golf field maker for putting hazards in the course. The game is enhanced by their very presence.

Why not take the hazards out of golf?

Authors who invent problems for courses in mathematics and science are not condemned by the public by placing such skill-developing obstacles in the mental pathways of our children. And how far would our writers of novels and authors of success magazine articles be without their stories of young men and women who started as "greenhorns" and grew to influence and power through their heroic struggles against seemingly insurmountable obstacles?

Then why should we so often blame the Creator and worry ourselves into frantic disposition because we find ourselves faced with suffering and persecution, than which no better hills could be found for the development of powerful, spiritual lives? It may help us to see the possibility of such growth if we note a few practical, everyday examples of playing the game.

A high school boy was tormented by one of his teachers. For some reason she seemed to hold a grudge against him. One day when he took his books home from school, he declared that he would not study again. The teacher's unfair punishment was more than he could stand. But he was persuaded by a wise father to think of her not so much as a curse, but as a blessing. She could prove his downfall or she could be his hill for the development of a strong personality. He finally chose to make her the latter. During the year in which she ruffled him the wrong way, he made it an opportunity to strengthen his patience, for he said, "This is my hill for the building of great courage and determination." And when the year had passed a boy of flexible disposition had developed a rounded, powerful personality, because he had climbed the hill and had breathed his spiritual lungs full of oxygen.

"I once knew a student who took delight in criticizing every lesson I ever gave," said a certain teacher. "No matter how poorly or how well I delivered my material, I could always tell, if not by his words, at least by his facial expressions that he was tearing my lesson to pieces. Then came the idea, why not make him my hill to climb? If he causes me to be angry, then I am weak in that particular area. If he discourages me, then I need greater determination. After that, whenever I met him or saw his critical face in the audience, I threw back my shoulders and said to myself, "There's my hill. Get ready to climb!' "

"The result has been that I have discovered some of his criticisms to be justified, and I have developed my own teaching ability in a considerable degree. He has actually helped me to be a stronger teacher because I used his criticism as a means of climbing to greater heights and greater strength of mind and heart. It proved to me, once and for all, the logic of Jesus' statement: "Blessed are ye, when men shall revile you, and persecute you, . . . for my sake. Rejoice, and be exceeding glad." (Matt. 5:11-12, and 3 Nephi 12:11-12.)

I remember reading of a medical missionary in China who was at work in his hospital one day when soldiers of Chiang Kai-shek's army approached and began the destruction of his building. As the missionary stood later and viewed the remains of the hospital into which he had put so much of his labor, he was tempted to find some method of revenge. But the longer he thought over the problem, the more convinced he was that the best way to take vengeance was to do good. He had been persecuted, but he would now use the persecution as a hill to climb in the spreading of his medical talents and good works. He followed the army and offered his serv- ices in taking care of the wounded soldiers of the Chiang Kai-shek's army. Day after day he worked with them and gave himself untiringly and sympathetically to the task of relieving their suffering. And later, after Chiang Kai- shek had become a Christian, his wife declared that one of the reasons for his conversion was the impression that was made upon him by the loving deeds of this medical missionary, who had used his persecution for good instead of evil.

Exactly why do the righteous suffer. The scriptures do not always tell us. If we would take a suggestion from Job's experience, we would not need to worry about the problem. No one has all of the answers. Besides, if we believe that God is all-powerful and all-wise and all- merciful, there is no particular reason why we should not trust him to handle the world in the right way. The Lord is very clear concerning two points: he lets us understand that if we do anything worthwhile, we will be persecuted; and he intimates that such persecution may either cause our downfall or prove the very means of developing stronger character and greater personality.

Some day we may know exactly whether God purposely puts these ugly hills in our paths or whether, like Topsy, they "just grew up" as a result of our free agency and we just happened to run into them. The important thing at present is to take Jesus' caution and climb them with a smile. The temptation will be to wish that we could be freed from trouble and persecution. Jesus would have us know that it is better to rejoice and be exceedingly glad; or as the Book of Mormon suggests, ". . . men are, that they might have joy." (2 Nephi 2:25). "For so persecuted they the prophets which were before you." (Matt. 5: 12, and 3 Nephi 12:12.)

REFLECTIONS ON MAKING THE BEST USE OF YOUR TALENTS

Life means my opportunity to serve humanity.

—FRITZ KREISLER

A gentleman is one who puts more into life than he takes out of it.

—GEORGE BERNARD SHAW

I know of no great man except those who have rendered great service to the human race.

—VOLTAIRE

The aristocracy of today is not one of birth or wealth, but of those who do things for the welfare of their fellowmen.

—CHARLES M. SCHWAB

I give it as my firmest conviction that service to a just cause rewards the worker with more real happiness and satisfaction than any other venture of life.

—CARRIE CHAPMAN CATT

That company which renders service efficiently and satisfactorily is following the surest path to financial success.

—JOHN D. ROCKEFELLER, JR.

There is no happiness in mere dollars. After they are acquired, one can use but a very moderate amount . . . the greatest good a man can do is to cultivate himself, develop his powers, in order that he may be of greater service to humanity.

—MARSHALL FIELD

CHAPTER VII

MAKE THE BEST USE
OF YOUR TALENTS

In the scriptures we read about the "talent" principle of successful living. What is this principle taught by the Savior?

"Ye are the salt of the earth," he said to his followers. (Matt. 5:13, and 3 Nephi 12:13.) Why did he compare them to salt? For one thing, salt achieves its greatest purpose when it flavors, preserves, and brings life to other food without being conspicuous. Food without salt is flat and unsavory, but food with too much seasoning is even worse.

From the frying pan into the "ire".

So it is with people. For example, many leaders in almost every field fail for no other reason than that they have made themselves more prominent than the cause they were trying to promote. A prominent coach at one of our great universities has said, "The best football players I have known are those who throw themselves into the game with no thought of personal glory but with the supreme purpose of helping their team to win."

One writer has suggested, "There is almost no limit to the good we can do if we do not care who gets the credit." The Savior intimated that this principle would work for each of us, whatever our situation. "Whosoever will save his life shall lose it: but whosoever will lose his life for my sake, the same shall save it." (Luke 9:24.) "Ye are the salt of the earth," and you gain your greatest advantage and do your best work when you flavor and give life to the world without making yourself conspicuous.

In the time of Jesus, people thought of salt not only as a means of flavoring and preserving food but also as having a mysterious, life-giving property. Remember, for example, the Arabian Nights' story of the man who killed another person, cut his body in many places, rubbed salt into his wounds, and hid him in a cave, only to find later that the salt had brought him back to life.

This early connotation of salt has carried over into such present-day expressions as "Mr. So-andSo has more salt than his neighbor," meaning he has more vim and enthusiasm—more life. Instead of calling a person "the life of the party," people would think of him as "the salt of the party." (I wish that some of my long-faced teachers had had this interpretation.) To serve as dedicated Latter-day Saints does not mean we have to be killjoys. Jesus advised us to "rejoice and be exceeding glad." He would have us be the salt—the life, the joy givers, the enthusiasm generators—of the world.

Jesus also said to his disciples, "Ye are the light of the world." (Matt. 5:14, and 3 Nephi 12:14.) He did not call his disciples "light fixtures"; he called them *lights*. There is a vast difference, as one community discovered recently when a flood rendered the town's lighting system powerless. Not knowing the reason for the difficulty, many inhabitants examined their light fuses and attempted to put the light fixtures into good condition, but still the lights did not come on. The trouble was not with the fixtures—it was with the current that should have come through the mechanical apparatus to produce the light.

Have you ever wondered if people and constructive organizations sometimes fool themselves into thinking they have many beautiful lights, when in reality they have mainly light fixtures? Attractive? Yes, they provide decoration for some occasions. But what our confused communities need—what the bewildered world must have to help it out of its darkened condition—is more light, not more decoration.

"Ye are the light of the world. A city that is set on an hill cannot be hid. Neither do men light a candle, and put it under a bushel, but on a candlestick; and it giveth light unto all that are in the house. Let your light so shine before men, that they may see your good works, and glorify your Father which is in heaven." (Matt. 5:14-16, and 3 Nephi 12:14-16.) The following story is a true account of a group of men who took seriously these words of counsel from the Savior.

A large corporation in an eastern city was failing to make a good impression on its worldwide customer trade. When the chairman of the board of directors died and it came time to select a successor, fifty men of the

company scouted the nation and chose the most capable
man they could find. But after the new chairman had
served for a year, conditions were no better than before.
Even with great ideas and much enthusiasm, there was
little or no change in the volume of sales and net profit.

Unable to understand the situation, the fifty men met
again. After hours of discussion, they were finally
brought to their senses by one of their salesmen who said,
"Gentlemen, you know as well as I that in order to sell a
product successfully, you must do two things: first, get a
good product, and second, tell the world about it. Have
we a product that is worth telling the world about? If so,
let's get busy and tell the world."

A motion was quickly made, seconded, and passed;
these fifty men agreed to use the many channels of communication to tell everybody, far and near, about their
organization and its many useful products. A year later
it was necessary for the corporation to expand its opera-
tions to accommodate the new demand.

Helpful as such methods may be, they do not help us

achieve the greatest capacity of our lives until, in the words of Paul, we present our "bodies a living sacrifice, holy, acceptable unto God, which is [our] reasonable service." (Romans 12:1.) If ours is a gift of money, let it be a *living* gift. Let it not be something that we can give without noticing it, but rather a sum for which we dig deep into our lives, one that takes from us that which we would much rather have kept for ourselves.

The Savior praised the poor widow who gave all that she had. (Mark 12:42-44.) When a person can fast or pay his tithes without noticing the difference, he has given only a dead gift. It becomes a living sacrifice, whether large or small, only when it takes from the individual that which he really needs or greatly desires for himself.

If we render service, let it also be taken from our lives. Helping only when it is convenient and cooperating in worthy projects merely because we have nothing else to do can hardly be considered living contributions. We give our best service when we are first dedicated to that cause we serve.

I think of a soldier friend of mine in World War II. All of his close associates in his squad were killed by a mortar blast. Though wounded himself, he refused help until he accomplished his mission. For several hours he rode through the midst of bombs and slaughter, experiencing much personal anxiety and suffering, but he did not leave the battle line. From the concluding words of a letter he wrote to a friend, we may sense his courageous, unselfish spirit: "One may even get used to dying, if he dies a sufficient number of times."

It would be well for us to remember that there are many kinds of light, and many places from which to shine them. The fact that someone is not doing what other people are doing is not always a sign that he is not following Jesus' principle of service. A boy scout told his scoutmaster one night that he had been unable to do a good turn that day. When asked why, he replied, "You see, my dad is sick, and I had to be with him nearly all day long. I had to run several errands for him. Often I had to go to his bed to answer his calls. I read to him for a little while and even tried to write a couple of letters for him. All of it took so much time that I didn't have a chance to do my good turn."

Perhaps it is in such informal ways as this that many of us must let our lights shine. An attractive young woman remained unmarried for twenty-five years, in order to be of greater service to her mother. She may or may not have done the right thing as the church or world would judge, but she felt that it was her way to do a good turn. A friend of mine who is a doctor gives several hours a day to the care of patients who have no means to pay. And two good women I know spend one morning each week visiting homeless patients in a senior citizen sanitarium.

A certain businessman believes one of his chief tasks is helping young people get a proper start in the business world. Almost every time I talk with him, he tells me enthusiastically about some of his clerks whom he has helped to a better understanding of their work. Another leading businessman gives himself untiringly to the building of a better community life. He has no desire to hold political offices, and he seeks for no personal glory. He fights evil. He campaigns for honest men. At every turn he uses his influence to promote justice and the spirit of good will. Without thought of material reward for himself or his family, he takes delight in letting his light shine wherever it can be used to good advantage.

We need more like him.

Other simple and practical forms of service are suggested in the teachings and example of Jesus. "When thou makest a dinner or a supper, call not thy friends, nor thy brethren, neither thy kinsmen, nor thy rich neighbors; lest they also bid thee again, and a recompence be made thee. But when thou makest a feast, call the poor, the maimed, the lame, the blind: And thou shalt be blessed; for they cannot recompense thee: . . . I was an hungered, and ye gave me meat: I was thirsty, and ye gave me drink: I was a stranger, and ye took me in: Naked, and ye clothed me: I was sick, and ye visited me: I was in prison, and ye came unto me . . . Inasmuch as ye have done it unto one of the least of these my brethren, ye have done it unto me." (Luke 14:12-14, and Matt. 25:35-36, 40.)

Jesus had much to say about the use of wealth. He received help from well-to-do people; and so far as we can tell, it was not the possession but the wrong use of money that he fought against. "And one of the company said unto him, Master, speak to my brother, that he divide the inheritance with me . . . And he said unto them, Take heed, and beware of covetousness: for a man's life consisteth not in the abundance of the things which he possesseth." (Luke 12:13,15.) When a rich, young man came asking for advice, Jesus said, "One thing thou lackest: go thy way, sell whatsoever thou hast, and give to the poor, . . . and follow me." (Mark 10:21.) He did not condemn the man as a sinner because he had valuable things. Knowing the young man's great wealth and realizing his need for spiritual exercise, Jesus told him to sell what he had and to give to the poor. Christ was not attempting to give a solution to all our economic problems; he was answering the rich man's question concerning the betterment of his life.

Jesus knew that it was difficult to build a great spiritual life and a great fortune at the same time. "How hard is it for them that trust in riches to enter into the kingdom of God! It is easier for a camel to go through the eye of a needle, than for a rich man to enter into the kingdom of God." (Mark 10:24-25.) Whether the needle's eye refers to a small gate or a small hole does not really matter; Jesus was using a large object and a small passage to show by hyperbole how impossible it is for the one to go through the other. Probably remembering some very generous, rich people of his acquaintance, Jesus added, "With men it is impossible, but not with God: for with God all things are possible." (Mark 10:27.)

Jesus took time to be thoughtful of the needs of children; he painted a black picture for one who put a stumbling block in their way. Tobacco advertisers, liquor companies, movie producers and magazine publishers who, for the sake of personal gain, place suggestive crime and sex-filled pictures before the pliable minds of youth, take stock of yourselves! And you who go to church and talk much about the beauty of brotherly love on Sunday and then, in the presence of children during the rest of the week, talk loudly about the faults of your neighbors—you, too, examine your hearts!

Jesus lifted women from a secondary position in life and placed them on a plane of equality with men. He openly confessed his confidence in people who lacked confidence. He gave dignity and a new sense of personal worth to publicans and sinners by disregarding social customs and going to their homes for dinner. Every day it was the same. With no sounding trumpet to advertise his humanitarian spirit and in a simple, friendly fashion, he went about the world doing good.

Is it any wonder that intelligent men and ignorant men, strong men and weak men, professional leaders and manual laborers, sinners and saints—is it any wonder that men and women from all races, classes, and stations of life have bowed their knees and raised their voices before the divine Son of Man, this carpenter of Nazareth? Yet he was only putting into practice the principles he has revealed to us since the beginning of time, the principles that he has said will bring success to any who will follow where they lead.

With more power than anyone before and since his time has ever possessed, Christ was and is the most humble of all. He placed righteousness above material possessions and physical comfort; he was merciful even toward those who hated him. He constantly confused his enemies by his clear, unprejudiced thinking; he was an enthusiastic peacemaker, sowing always in his teaching those seeds of truth that would eventuate some day in harmonious living. He rejoiced in his opportunity to suffer for a good cause; and he served his fellowmen as salt that inconspicuously flavors and gives life to food and as a light that shines upon a hill to those who otherwise would sit in darkness.

He lived a helpful, unselfish life, and he advised those who wanted to know the joy of abundant living to follow his example. Only through such experience may we have an opportunity for the fullest expression of our better selves. When salt no longer fulfills the function of salt, it is "good for nothing, but to be cast out, and to be trodden under foot of men." (Matt. 5:13, and 3 Nephi 12:13.)

When a light refuses to shine, it is no longer a light. There is a difference between light fixtures and the light they are supposed to produce. And when we, as the creations of an unselfish, sacrificial Heavenly Father, as members of the Church of his Divine Son, and as members of a society in which each person is dependent in greater or lesser degree upon the cooperation and contribution of others—when we refuse to give, we deny the natural function of the human soul.

Summing the whole matter up in a single sentence, particularly as it applies to successful living, Jesus said, "Whosoever will be great among you, let him be your minister; And whosoever will be chief among you, let him be your servant." (Matt. 20:26-27.) This law of life promises failure to those who seek to avoid the principle and assures happiness and eternal joy to all who will follow where it leads.

REFLECTIONS ON THE VALUE
OF BEING YOUR OWN BOSS

I will allow no man to drag me downhill by making me hate him.

—BOOKER T. WASHINGTON

Govern thyself, and you will be able to govern the world

—CHINESE PROVERB

No man, resolved to make the most of himself, can spare time for personal contention. Still less can he afford to take all the consequences, including the vitiating of his temper and the loss of self-control.

—ABRAHAM LINCOLN

Gentlemen use heart; lesser men use strength.

—CHINESE PROVERB

Democracies can stand securely only on one foundation—good will to men: good will to all men. Tyrannies may endure for a time on the basis of ill will to men: race against race, language against language, class against class. But no tyranny endures forever.

—ALVIN JOHNSON

Character survives; goodness lives; love is immortal.

—ROBERT G. INGERSOLL

Eye hath not seen, nor ear heard, neither have entered into the heart of man, the things which God hath prepared for them that love him.

—I CORINTHIANS 2:9

CHAPTER VIII

BE YOUR OWN BOSS

Someone has said, "The measure of a man is the size of the things that make him angry." This truism is illu-

The measure of a man.

103

strated in the life and teachings of the Savior, as well as in the lives of other noble souls.

Although Jesus warned his disciples against the evil results of uncontrolled temper, he sometimes became angry himself, so angry once that he prepared to use force if necessary, to drive evil practice from the temple. (John 2:15.) But consider, if you will, the size of the things that aroused his anger. Man called him the prince of devils, and he paid little attention to their insult. They spat in his face, mocked and hit him, and even hung him to the cross, but he did not lose control of his feelings.

It was quite different, however, when the Pharisees criticized him for doing good on the Sabbath. Realizing that the Sabbath was made for man, and not man for the Sabbath, Christ had healed a man with a withered hand on the sacred day; and when he found the crowd in a critical mood, the Savior "looked round about on them with anger." (Mark 3:5.)

As long as men ridiculed him personally, Christ ignored them. But in the presence of injustice, when men were unfair and unkind to each other, Jesus threw the influence of his great, tempered personality against their evil practices. No one could hurt him by attempting to punish him on the outside. But when they were cruel to each other, they touched his heart.

Another great soul became so angry as he watched a crowd of selfish, narrow-minded people selling slaves that he swore if he ever had the chance, he would hit that practice and hit it hard. Unruffled by small or bitter talk about himself, Abraham Lincoln had more than a sufficient amount of tempered ammunition to turn loose on deeds of social injustice. Every American school child knows how hard, and with what wonderful results, Lincoln attacked the practice of slavery when he finally had his chance.

Coming farther down the road of history, one sees a young immigrant boy stepping onto the shores of the United States. He had had no education. He was so poor that he was compelled to sleep in streets and alleys and to eat scraps from a restaurant table. One day when he was older and employed as a newspaper reporter, he walked into a tenement in New York City. He asked the mother of a large family, all of whom lived in one room, if they ever had any fresh air.

"We have a window opening into the airpassage of the building."

"Do you have any sunlight?"

"About three times a year the sun manages to shine on the upper part of one of our walls."

Outraged, the one-time immigrant boy threw the weight of his tempered personality against this terrible injustice. Year after year he printed pictures of the awful slum conditions and wrote illuminating articles to stir the thinking of the good people of the city. For ten years Jacob Riis kept at the task before the citizens were sufficiently awakened to the injustice to pass laws against the worst type of tenements.

Jesus, Abraham Lincoln, and Jacob Riis were not tempestuous; they were tempered. Paying no heed to the thousand and one slights and disappointments that would have caused most people to lose control of themselves, these great souls spent their emotion and energy in well-focused battles against those forces that seek to destroy social values. If we are big enough, will there not be times when we will fight with righteous indignation against the unbrotherly conduct of selfish people?

But, let us not confuse the well-controlled use of

unselfish enthusiasm with the raucous roaring of a weak, tempestuous spirit. In the life and philosophy of the Savior there is a definite place for the former; there is neither time nor place for the latter. "Ye have heard that it was said by them of old time, Thou shalt not kill; and whosoever shall kill shall be in danger of the judgment." (Matt. 5:21-22, and 3 Nephi 12:21-22.)

Don't carry a chip on your shoulder.

Some scholars have translated this passage to mean "whosoever maligns his brother." Luccock goes on to expound these verses, "When we malign, we have venom. Maligning is a branch of the art of murder. And it is here linked up with the punishment for murder. It murders reputation and influence, both of which are sacred, inseparable parts of personality. When men malign, they murder by poison, the most cowardly type of murder. . . . We can malign by insinuations, which are much like arsenic, in that it is hard to establish positive guilt. . . . The most deadly way of maligning is to misstate, either carelessly or with malice, another's position. He is rarely able to refute." (H. Luccock, *Values in New Translations of the New Testament,* p. 17.)

Jesus also says, "Ye have heard that it hath been said, An eye for an eye, and a tooth for a tooth: But I say unto you, That ye resist not evil: but whosoever shall smite thee on thy right cheek, turn to him the other also." (Matt. 5:38-39, and 3 Nephi 12:38-39.) Jesus did not confront persecution when it was unnecessary. He made his final trip to Jerusalem only when he felt he could no longer stay away. Nor was he in the habit of telling people to strike him again after they had once spat upon him or hit him. Evidently his statement which we have just quoted is not so much a law as a principle of life, suggesting that a non-combative spirit is preferable to a cantankerous attitude that insists upon wearing a chip on the shoulder and always looking for revenge.

Jesus believed that the best way to do away with anger and hatred was to put love in their place. However, the Greek words that have been translated into English as "love" do not always mean the same thing. "Ye have heard that it hath been said, Thou shalt love thy neighbor, and hate thine enemy. But I say unto you, Love your enemies, . . . and pray for them which despitefully use you, and persecute you; That ye may be the children of your Father which is in heaven." (Matt. 5:43-45, and 3 Nephi 12:43-45.) Could a man love the murderer of his father as much, for instance, as he would love his own wife or children? Such would undoubtedly be impossible for any of us. And, according to some of the best authorities, Jesus gave no such advice.

The Greek word that is translated "love" in this case is "agape" which the Greek dictionary defines as "to wish well to, to take pleasure in." Thus, while we cannot be absolutely sure of the full meaning that Jesus had in mind when he said, "Love your enemies," we can be fairly certain that he was advising the expression of a spirit of good will—and not much more than that. Evidently Jesus felt that this was something everyone could do if he tried hard enough. If, instead of hating our enemies, we would love them and pray for them, if we would try our best to hold good feelings toward them and to have the spirit of good will, he promised we would be children of our Heavenly Father. Christ concluded his thoughts on love and nonresistance with this challenge: "Be ye therefore perfect, even as your Father which is in heaven is perfect." (Matt. 5:48, and 3 Nephi 12:48.)

One might say, "A beautiful theory—this business of controlling one's temper and trying to be thoughtful of everyone's welfare, even that of your enemies. But does it work?" We talk about it, but few people are willing to try it. What can it accomplish? Someone has suggested, "If only love is life, and man is made from love, then every bit of hate in me works for death; every bit of love works for life."

I recall sitting in an educational psychology class some years ago at the University of Southern California when a noted psychologist made this statement: "It isn't your nerves that set you on edge; it's your lack of emotional balance. You can almost be certain that your cause for 'collapse' is wrapped up in problems defying solution, in some 'blocking' that you cannot overcome. . . . If your emotions constantly upset your glandular and other organic functions in such a way that your bloodstream can't purify, you bid for a position that may result in serious illness." Almost any reputable scientist will tell you that jealousy, fear, hate, and rage are among the worst poisons that one may harbor in his mind, and as such they are very detrimental to physical health.

Uncontrolled anger affects one's ability to think clearly; for example: a husband and wife arguing heatedly over some problem of the home; opponents in politics or religion fighting, with waving arms and violent words, over some party issue; capitalists and laborers struggling under the excitement of strike conditions to arrive at some self-valued settlement; baseball players on two sides of an umpire's decision; or angered contestants in a court trial. Could anyone really expect people under such conditions to think intelligently and reasonably?

Like some cruel, merciless monster, anger and hatred

often collect their toll for the rest of a person's natural life. A few moments of thought and a little extra effort to control words and actions that spring from momentary anger may save one from a sorrow that time and repentance might never eradicate. As Will Careton graphically pictures it,

Boys flying kites haul in their white-winged birds;
You can't do that way when you're flying words; . . .

Thoughts unexpressed may sometimes fall back dead;
But God himself can't kill them when they're said.

At the time of small difficulties, a spirit of good will, enthusiastically exercised, will often keep us from getting into more serious trouble. Said the Savior: "Therefore if thou bring thy gift to the altar, and there rememberest that thy brother hath ought against thee; Leave there thy gift before the altar, and go thy way; first be reconciled to thy brother, and then come and offer thy gift." (Matt. 5:23-24, and 3 Nephi 12:23-24.)

How do you face up to your differences?

Before going on to the next verses, let us recall some of the conditions and customs of Palestine. There were few judges in the days of the Savior, so when two men quarreled and felt that they must go to a judge, which was the common practice, they were often compelled to walk long distances to reach the city in which the judge was located. Because there were many bandits in the country who would just as soon kill them as look at them, the two opponents, even though they often hated each other, would go together across country in order to protect themselves.

Quite naturally, as they traveled day after day, they would begin to talk; and through their conversation, each often decided that the other person was not so bad as he had thought. In such a case, the two would sometimes return without meeting the judge. However, if they did not agree along the way, the judge might decide that this was a good opportunity to make a profit. If he found that they had wealth or came from wealthy families, the judge would probably turn them over to an officer and have them jailed until they had paid their last farthing.

With this information in mind, we are now ready to see the application of Jesus' very practical advise. If you begin a journey to see the judge about your difficulties, "agree with thine adversary quickly, whiles thou art in the way with him; lest at any time the adversary deliver thee to the judge, and the judge deliver thee to the officer, and thou be cast into prison. Verily I say unto thee, Thou shalt by no means come out thence, till thou hast paid the uttermost farthing." (Matt. 5:25-26, and 3 Nephi 12:25-26.)

Is not that the very essence of common sense? I remember a successful businessman in Los Angeles one day making the statement that he would be willing to go to church if the ministers could tell him anything that would help solve his daily problems. Could anyone want advice more practical than the statement of Jesus that we have just read? Think of the law suits that could be avoided, the energy, health, and peace of mind that could be saved, if people could be sensible enough to settle their little difficulties before they became monstrous, devastating, almost unsolvable problems.

One thinks of the trite, but very true, expression, "Of all sad words of tongue or pen, the saddest are these: it might have been." Sometimes two people, who might have exercised a little patience in a heated moment and remained the best of friends, have fallen prey to the misery and the heartache of a life-long feud because they surrendered their intellect to a fickle temper. "Verily I say unto thee, Thou shalt by no means come out thence, till thou hast paid the uttermost farthing." (Matt. 5:26, and 3 Nephi 12:26.)

Love actually wins battles in its contest with anger and rage. A plant manager of a large manufacturing firm told me that for years he had been an unhappy failure in his job. None of his men liked him, and none of them wanted to do what he asked. "But," he said, "the reason was because I tried to force them to do what I wanted, and I constantly lost my temper when they refused to act immediately upon my command. When told by my superior officer that I would lose my position unless I could do better, I decided to try the suggestion of the Savior. I started by speaking in a friendly voice to everyone in the building. I allowed my men to make suggestions. I never became angry; I worked sympathetically with all who worked under me. And the result was almost beyond my fondest hopes. It really worked. I wouldn't go back to the old method for anything in the world!"

Love is always the winner.

One young religious educator was always ready to fight with anyone who disagreed with him. Then he was faced with a real crisis in his program. Three of his leading students had come to despise him and did all they could to have him removed. When disaster came into their homes and he went to visit them, they called him "liar, cheat," and many other unpleasant names. "But," he said, "I decided to try the Savior's plan. Clenching my fists in my pocket and holding my temper as I never had before, I said only kind words in return. On numerous occasions they snubbed me, and although there was not the slightest change in their attitude for several years, I kept trying to be kind. Then one day the wedges of love entered into their hearts of steel, and animosity was blown to the winds. My enemies became three of my loyal friends, willing to do anything that I asked of them, and anxious always to serve in the interest of building the kingdom."

In the battle between hatred and love, hatred will undoubtedly win many of the early battles. But in the long run, Jesus would have us believe that love will be the victor—it was around this conviction that he built his own philosophy of life and established the plan of salvation. Indignation on behalf of one's fellowmen brings progress, destroying prejudice, superstition, and social injustice. Indignation against one's fellows, especially when it is of the poisonous variety, inevitably proves a menace toward all concerned, not only endangering the peace of the one hated, but also weakening the physical health and thinking ability of the one who hates, placing upon the memory scars that may never be erased, causing the growth of foolish and needless enmity, and making certain the final failure in one's struggle for the abundant life.

The Savior spoke not only as a religionist, but as the voice of divine and human experience when he told us to be tempered not tempestuous, to fight against evil deeds, even among our friends, and to love everybody, even our enemies.

REFLECTIONS ON THE VALUE OF HONESTY

Every man should make up his mind that if he expects to succeed, he must give an honest return for the other man's dollar.

—EDWARD H. HARRIMAN

An ounce of loyalty is worth a pound of cleverness.

—ELBERT HUBBARD

A politician thinks of the election; a statesman of the next generation.

—JAMES FREEMAN CLARK

No man has a good enough memory to make a successful liar.

—ABRAHAM LINCOLN

I should say sincerity, a deep, great, genuine sincerity, is the first characteristic of all men in any way heroic.

—CARLYLE

Who is the greater criminal, the man who pays in counterfeit money or the man who accepts pay for counterfeit work.

—LOS ANGELES TIMES

Salesmanship consists in bringing to the buyer something he needs at a profitable price. A persuasive tongue is a poor substitute for knowledge and honesty.

—ANONYMOUS

Only faith that the universe is keyed to truth, that it braces and supports and gives ultimate victory to the truth, will keep our souls free from the taint of pessimism.

—ANONYMOUS

CHAPTER IX

BE HONEST

A young man surrendered a good position because he discovered that his employers were dishonest. The employers said nothing at the time. But after a few days they sent for the young man and offered him a substantial increase in salary if he would come back to his old job. Though dishonest themselves, they appreciated dependability in others and were willing to pay a good price to obtain it in their clerks.

"Is it ever right to tell a lie?" The question has been debated from time immemorial by the best and worst of students. Even today there are many people on both sides of the argument. Some contend that one is justified in making false statements when dealing with mentally incompetent people, with patients who are seriously ill, or with an enemy in time of war. Some maintain that it is better to be dishonest than unkind; "Whenever the truth hurts the other fellow or does unwarranted injury to yourself, tell a lie and go to sleep with an easy conscience." But Richard C. Cabot, professor of social ethics and clinical medicine at Harvard University some years ago, took a different view of the problem. In his book, *The Meaning of Right and Wrong,* he said:

> It appears to me, therefore, that the doctrine that it is sometimes right to lie can never be effectively asserted. For our hearers take notice, and so make ineffective our subsequent attempts to lie. I recall a sick man who ordered his physician never to tell him the truth in case he should be seriously ill. Picture the

Is it ever right to tell a lie?

state of that sick man's mind when later he hears his physician's reassurances . . . Whatever the doctor does or says, his patient has grounds of fearing the worst. No reassurance can be taken at its face value. The most trifling ailment must be suspect; good news may always mean bad . . . So far as I can see, then, the conscientious defense of lying is impossible. (Richard C. Cabot, *The Meaning of Right and Wrong,* p. 167-168.)

Whichever side we may take in the argument, whether or not we are always truthful ourselves, experience shows that we still have more confidence in one whom we can trust to speak and act with integrity. Whom can we trust? The salesman of a commodity which we need but which we know little about? The person with whom we have decided to enter a business or professional partnership? The contractor to whom we have given the full responsibility of building our new house? Our physician deciding upon the question of a serious operation? Whoever it is, and whatever our relationship with him may be, we go farther with the one we can completely trust.

The great composer Beethoven said he would not have a housekeeper who lied to spare him annoyance. "Whoever tells a lie is not clean-hearted, and such a person cannot cook a clean meal."

John Galsworthy, prominent English novelist, says: "Honesty in thought and speech and written word is a jewel, and they who curb prejudice and seek honorably to know and speak the truth are the only true builders of a better life."

In a booklet entitled "How to Study and Like It," two teachers at the University of Washington some years ago asked their students some thought-provoking questions. "How would you like to have your appendix taken out by a surgeon who cheated his way through medical school? Or drive an automobile over a bridge built by an engineer who cheated in his exams on engineering?"

Former chairman of the board of the United States Steel Corporation, Albert H. Gray, tells others how to succeed in business, contending that "a man, whatever his occupation, should be absolutely honest. Akin to honesty is accuracy in representation and statement. . . . Business is one of the biggest things in the world. And honesty is surely the biggest thing in business."

A highly successful business executive says, "The question most frequently asked me by salesmen is how I have been able to get the biggest financial, industrial, railroad, and mercantile leaders in America to open up and talk with me unreservedly. Briefly, you must earn a reputation for unimpeachable truthfulness, for accuracy, for fairness, and for knowing your job. Win the confidence of one leader in any line, and he will gladly recommend that others not be afraid to have dealings with you. One of the richest men in the world gave me, as the most important step to success: 'First earn a credit, a character, a reputation.' "

Token of my self esteem.

Is it any wonder that the Savior, who knew life and the rules of life better than anyone else, should place a strong emphasis upon this fundamental principle of honesty? He did not say a man would be cast out because he told a lie. Jesus insisted that he had come to the world in order that we "might have life, and . . . might have it more abundantly." (John 10:10.) He spent much of his time stressing the principles by which each of us can build for ourselves a successful, abundant life.

Jesus advised us, if we want to be certain of the best in life, to be open-minded, energetic in our desire for righteousness, merciful, clear thinking, a peacemaker instead of a troublemaker, loyal to a great cause even at the expense of persecution, unselfish, in control of our emotions at all times, and—honest. But how honest would he have us be?

The Lord said that we should be so honest that we could express an opinion by the simple words "Yes" or "No," so that people would know exactly where we stood. Jesus' idea of simple, open-faced honesty was a far cry from the complicated, scheming methods of the early Hebrew people. Remember, for example, the case of Jacob and Laban. Jacob made a contract with his uncle Laban to work seven years in order to marry his daughter. But Laban tricked him into marrying the wrong girl. Jacob, in turn, played a clever game by which he secured practically all of Laban's good flocks. Angered, the uncle sought Jacob's life, so Jacob fled, taking flocks and family from the reach of Laban's power. (Gen. 29-31.)

This is only one of many similar cases which could be cited in the Old Testament, showing the attitude of the Hebrew people toward honesty before and at the time of Christ. The Hebrews did have one effective check on dishonesty. When accused of telling a lie, modern children say, "I cross my heart and hope to die." With practically the same motive in mind, the Hebrews made an oath that what they were saying was true. Sometimes they swore by the footstool of God, sometimes by the hair of their heads, or by numerous other things which were accepted as sufficient guarantee of their truthful intentions. But they had to swear by something before their word would be accepted as the truth.

Then came the Savior with another philosophy of life. Seeing how men could not trust one another and how unstable the old system was bound to make society, Christ pushed it overboard and said very frankly and clearly, "Let your communication be, Yea, yea; Nay, nay: for whatsoever is more than these cometh of evil." (Matt. 5:37, and 3 Nephi 12:37.) It is useless to swear by anybody or anything. If a man were absolutely honest and everybody knew from experience with him that he could be trusted in word and deed, no other security would be needed but his word. I remember my father saying, "When you are dishonest, you counterfeit the circulating medium of society." And no individual or society can long continue successfully or harmoniously on a counterfeit basis.

That was what Jesus believed and taught. He had no use for a counterfeiter in religion or anywhere else. A person who is not willing to face the facts and pay the price of meeting the truth is a hypocrite, an undesirable citizen, and one who has enslaved himself and robbed himself of the birthright of a free and noble life. Honesty, with Jesus, was not only the best policy; it was and still is a necessary principle in the building of a just and dependable life.

If one doubts the value of the Savior's principle, let him think of the added stability that would come to society if every merchant were so honest that when he quoted the price and described the quality of his goods we could take him at his word; if every newspaper reporter would write so conscientiously that we could be sure to read the facts instead of propaganda; if when we read a personal recommendation that is brought to us, we could feel assured that the statements in the letter expressed the writer's honest opinion; if the words of praise that outstanding athletes and movie stars are reported to have given concerning advertised articles expressed their real attitudes and not something that they had been bought to write or say.

The question arises whether Jesus valued the principle of honesty enough to follow it constantly and rigidly in his own life. John records in his Gospel this quote from the Master: "To this end was I born, and for this cause came I into the world, that I should bear witness unto the truth." (John 18:37.) We know from the record that Jesus would not lie, even to save himself from the cross.

In all his dealings with the Jews, Christ's attitude was consistently one of straightforward honesty. Considering the Savior's passionate desire to have his revelation of the Father welcomed, his principles of life accepted in the private and social being of one man, one might think that Jesus would have been careful not to arouse the hostility of influential people. If he could have won over the rabbis, if he could have even persuaded them to neutrality, think how much easier his work would have been! The rabbis had prejudices; he could have trimmed his utterances, so as not to have aroused them. The Sadducees and Pharisees had characteristic sins; he could have spoken to them about something else. And he could have excused this attitude by saying that it was better for the acceptance of his message. But it was not so. The Lord's steadfast habit was to tell the plain truth, no matter whom he alienated.

If we are to judge by Jesus' example, we may know that lying consists not only of false speech, but also of disloyal silence. As some clever writer has said, "Silence is not always golden; sometimes it is just plain yellow." Not that a person should stick his neck into a noose and tell everything he knows for the sake of being virtuous—Jesus never invited danger by unnecessary bravery. But can you imagine him standing by with closed lips when a spoken word would have helped the reputation of another person?

A group of American men in China were criticizing the character of a well-known merchant. One condemned him for being a "cheat," another for handling a poor quality of goods, and another for not telling the truth. A motion was made to boycott him and do everything that could legally be done to make him close his store. Then a lone member of the group rose to his feet and suggested that before any such drastic action was taken, it might be a good idea to do some investigating. Accepting the advice, the men proceeded with the investigation. Much to the surprise of the majority of the group, the merchant in question was found to be a thoroughly reliable businessman. The evil some had heard about him was only gossip and had no foundation in fact. Instead of passing a motion to boycott the man, the group did an about face and proposed an effort to clear his good name. This is a case where silence on the part of the one member who knew the facts would have been both dishonest and disastrous.

Not only will a successful person be truthful and loyal in the words that he speaks, but also, according to Jesus, he will never display in public any religious act or custom that does not spring from the heart with genuine Christlike intent. Not only does it accomplish no good, it is actually dishonest to pray with one's lips word that do not originate sincerely in the heart. The same may be said of charity. As long as we give money to impress our fellow-

Ever double cross a friend?

men, we are nothing but hypocrites. If it is wrong for big businessmen to steal from other merchants, so it is wrong for us followers of the Savior to take mental and moral credit from others.

"Take heed that ye do not your alms before men, to be seen of them: otherwise ye have no reward of your Father which is in heaven. Therefore when thou doest thine alms, do not sound a trumpet before thee, as the hypocrites do in the synagogues and in the streets, that they may have glory of men. Verily I say unto you, They have their reward." (Matt. 6:1-2, and 3 Nephi 13:1-2.) No doubt, such people receive credit from some for their outward show, but such is cheap and fleeting remuneration. "But when thou doest alms, let not thy left hand know what thy right hand doeth: That thine alms may be in secret: and thy Father which seeth in secret himself shall reward thee openly." (Matt. 6:3-4, and 3 Nephi 13:3-4.)

Jesus would have us be so conscientious, so honest and above board in everything that we do and think, that we would not even attempt to show in the face any religious attitude we do not hold in the heart. "Moreover when ye fast, be not, as the hypocrites, of a sad countenance: for they disfigure their faces, that they may appear unto men to fast. Verily I say unto you, They have their reward." (Matt. 6:16, and 3 Nephi 13:16.) Let us not pretend that deception will not sometimes be rewarded. A lie, a crooked deal, a misrepresentation by false words, by silence, or by an outward display of humanitarian principles may often bring apparently good returns. But even from a selfish standpoint, one should realize that the quality of those "good" returns is very inferior to that which come to the person who day by day builds his life—in word and deed—according to the pattern of truth.

While Jesus admitted that one may get ahead through dishonest means, he taught that the one who holds tenaciously to these fundamental, God-given principles of life will reap the best possible results in character, personality, and general achievement. Speak falsely, give a harmful impression by your silence, make pretensions of great character when there are no great ideals within—in each instance you help build an unstable, undependable foundation for your life and for the whole human race. Be so honest and so sincere in all your thoughts, words, and actions that men will believe you, without the use of vows or other security. Thus you will take unto yourself such favor with God and with men, that yours will truly be an abundant life.

Phillips Brooks has caught the spirit of Jesus' teaching and has written it so simply and so impressively that we close the chapter with his admonition: "To keep clear of concealment, to keep clear of the need of concealment, to do nothing which he might not do out in the middle of Boston Common in the middle of noonday—I cannot say how more and more that seems to be the glory of a young man's life. It is an awful hour when the first necessity of hiding anything comes. Put off that day as long as possible. Put it off forever, if you can."

REFLECTIONS ON COURTESY

Cultivate courtesy as a business asset. . . . Meet rudeness with unfailing politeness and see how much better you feel.

—ELBERT HUBBARD

The tongue is but three inches long, but it can kill a man six feet high.

—JAPANESE AXIOM

Every man should keep a fair size cemetery in which to bury the faults of his friends.

—HENRY WARD BEECHER

I wholly disapprove of what you say and will defend to the death your right to say it.

—VOLTAIRE

Our oldest deacon ain't going to like heaven unless he is consulted as to the way it ought to be run.

—ANONYMOUS

It is ridiculous for any man to criticize the works of another if he has not distinguished himself by his own performances.

—ADDISON

Some people are so painfully good that they would rather be right than pleasant.

—C. BALL

A man's own good breeding is the best security against other people's ill manners. It carries along with it a dignity that is respected by the most petulant.

—ANONYMOUS

CHAPTER X

JUDGE NOT

One of the things that distinguished the Lord from other teachers and leaders of his time and since was his emphasis upon the proper attitudes behind one's deeds. Others had said that it was wrong to kill; Jesus insisted that one should not even be angry with his brother. Hebrew teachers had contended that one should not bear false witness; Jesus warned against the danger of holding mean and critical attitudes toward other people. "Judge not, that ye be not judged. For with what judgement ye judge, ye shall be judged: and with what measure ye mete, it shall be measured to you again." (Matt. 7:1-2, and 3 Nephi 14:1-2.)

After long experience, society has accepted certain rules of social behavior. Etiquette tells us how to respond graciously to an invitation, when to tip our hats, and how to address our superiors. I am sure Jesus would not object to many of these rules of etiquette. But, he would point out, unless you feel right toward your fellowmen on the inside, you will never know when your technical rules of etiquette, on the outside, are going to function in the proper way. If you are always careful to hold an intelligent and sympathetic attitude toward your fellowmen, you will seldom go wrong in your social life.

When shopping for a new automobile some years ago, I visited several agencies and talked with many different salesmen. One particularly impressed me as the most

What is more important than etiquette?

courteous salesman I had ever met. He pleasantly told
me everything I wanted to know about the car and did
not laugh when I asked foolish questions. He even allowed me to talk as much as I wanted without interrupt-
ing me—quite an exceptional, courteous salesman!

But a few days later when he learned that I had pur-
chased a car from another agency, he called me on the
telephone. He expressed doubt of my veracity, implied
certain ignorance on my part, and even suggested that I
had been unfair, ungracious, and almost everything else
that was unkind and uncomplementary. It was then I
realized that what he had shown me a few days before

had not been courtesy at all but merely an expression of pure selfishness.

I remembered seeing a sales book on his desk with the instructions, "The first thing to do in approaching a customer is to be courteous. The second thing to do is to be courteous. And the third thing to do is to be courteous." The smooth-talking salesman had memorized the message of these words and applied it mechanically in order to sell cars. When his vocal and facial display failed to accomplish his purpose, he dropped the curtain and revealed the "meaninglessness" and the hollowness of his inner life.

Do you remember what Jesus said about such people? He drew his simile from a graveyard scene. Describing the outward beauty of a tomb, he commented especially upon the artistic way it had been painted. But with all of its outward beauty, he pointed out that this tomb contained nothing within but dead men's bones—a picture perhaps of people who pay strict attention to formal rules and yet know nothing of the nature of true courtesy. Such people may be likened unto "whited sepulchres, which indeed appear beautiful outward, but are within full of dead men's bones, and of all uncleanness." (Matt. 23:27.)

To Jesus, courtesy meant something more than attractive deeds. What did it mean to him? How much courtesy would Jesus advise us to show in order to give and to gain the most in life?

During a visit to San Francisco after the terrible earthquake and fire, a writer saw a wealthy, cultured woman sitting on the pavement next to a poor uncultured man. The two of them were keeping comfortably warm because a blanket had been wrapped about them. Regardless of their different stations in life, at that particular moment they held no resentment toward one another. Through suffering, they found a common bond of kinship, which cut through artificial social classifications.

Note, however, a catastrophe was necessary before these two people became conscious of their common inheritance. But not so with the Savior; daily he regarded his fellowman with compassion. With sympathy and deep understanding, he easily pierced the traditional shell of social castes and found—not the rich and poor, not the learned and unlearned, not Greek or Roman, not Jew or Samaritan, but human beings with like hopes and aspirations—candidates, all of them, for the greater eternal family of God.

Think, for example, of Zacchaeus. A tax collector, he was a member of a group hated by the Jews. Many of these collectors not only took their rightful portion, but, when not sufficiently bribed, would also bring false witnesses to support the collector's claim that he had been tricked. The collector was then allowed to take approximately half of the grain that the accused farmers had produced.

Such behavior was characteristic of the class. Is it any wonder that the Jews hated tax collectors? No matter how good a man Zacchaeus himself might have been, the Jews regarded him as a legalized profiteer, a person unworthy of sympathetic treatment. Being a man of small stature and unable to see through the crowd, Zacchaeus climbed a tree to watch the Savior pass. When Jesus saw him, he looked upon the little man, not as a member of a group of tax collectors, but as an individual soul who had great aspirations and longings of his own. And seeing him as such, Jesus said unto him, "Zacchaeus, make haste, and come down; for today I must abide at thy house." (Luke 19:5.) In the custom of Palestine, to abide in another's home was an expression of personal appreciation and friendship.

To the Jews, an adultress was also a member of a certain class. According to law, these people deserved nothing better than to be stoned to death. But to the Savior, the woman taken in adultery was an individual who had made a tragic mistake, but who still had the opportunity of personal repentance. When she was accused before him, he did not embarrass her looking into her face. Instead he wrote upon the ground until all her accusers were gone. With great sympathy he then told her quietly to go her way and sin no more. (John 8:3-11.)

If we examine closely the Savior's advice to the woman, we will be able to appreciate more fully the impact of his words. "And the scribes and Pharisees brought into him a woman taken in adultery; and when they had set her in the midst, They say unto him, Master, this woman was taken in adultery, in the very act. Now Moses in the law commanded us, that such should be stoned: but what sayest thou? This they said, tempting him, that they might have to accuse him. But Jesus stooped down, and with his finger wrote on the ground, as though he heard them not. So when they continued asking him, he lifted up himself, and said unto them, He that is without sin among you, let him first cast a stone at her. And again he stooped down, and wrote on the ground. And they which heard it, being convicted by their own conscience, went out one by one, beginning at the eldest, even unto the last: and Jesus was left alone, and the woman stainding in the midst. When Jesus had lifted up himself, and saw none bu the woman, he said unto her, Woman, where are those thine accusers? hath no man condemned thee? She said, No man, Lord. And Jesus said unto her, Neither do I condemn thee: go, and sin no more." (John 8:3-11.)

Sin: to miss the mark.

Another social class that was bitterly hated by the
Hebrew people was the Samaritans, Jews whose blood
was mixed with that of other nations. But Jesus did not
classify people into groups. When he wanted to illustrate
the principle of courtesy and brotherly love, he told of a
certain Samaritan—who, when he found a hated Jew in
trouble—stepped across racial, geographic, economic,
and religious barriers to help a fellow human being.
(Luke 10:25-37.) A common person, of so little importance in his day that his name would not have even been
mentioned, yet his noble personality was immprtalized in
the simple act of loooking beyond man-made classifications and recognizing the inestimable worth of the human soul. Regardless of his station in life, this Samaritan
was a wonderful person.

The Jew had drawn a circle that shut him out,
Heretic, rebel, a thing to flout.
But a certain Samaritan had the courtesy to win,
He drew a circle that took him in.

Theology? Yes, very good theology. But also good
ethics of the seven-day-a-week variety. George Meredith
said:

See ye not, courtesy
Is the true alchemy,
Turning to gold all it touches and tries?

In teaching his son the value of courtesy, a merchant
said, "My boy, treat everybody with politeness, even
those who are rude to you. For remember, you show
courtesy to others not because they are gentlemen, but
because you are one."

When Booker T. Washington was denied a ride in a
taxicab by a white driver, Washington replied, "All right,
then, jump in yourself, and I will drive you." The white
man agreed, and at the end of the trip, Washington descended from the driver's seat and paid the full cost of
the ride.

We tip our hats to individual women on the street,
and we shake hands with individual men. But when
these same people seat themselves behind the steering
wheels of their automobiles, they immediately lose their
identity and become abstractions in the minds of most of
us. Would the teaching of the Savior have anything to
do with such mundane affairs as traffic jams and auto
accidents? Would conditions be improved if we could
look through the eyes of Christian courtesy when we
drive a car, if we thought of each person on the road as
an individual, as a brother or sister with as much right on
the road as we?

Some years ago one of the vice presidents of the National Safety Council said, "I am not joking when I say

bad manners are the cause of a great deal of traffic congestion. . . . All we have to do to improve traffic conditions is to use the same courtesy when driving that we display in our homes and offices. . . . Without spending a single cent we could cut down traffic congestion right now by observing the rules of decency and fair play when we drive. Give the other fellow a chance."

This principle has been proven in actual practice. Though the national average is something like one injury or death for every eighty-five thousand miles of driving, the Eastern Transit Company completed more than a million miles without a single injury or a cent of property damage. How? The manager explained, "Just taught my boys to be polite. In two years, in over two and a half million miles they have been involved in only two minor mishaps."

We need to extricate the individual from the mass and recognize his values as a human soul with rights and needs and aspirations of his own. This, however, is only a start. To follow Jesus' example and teaching, no matter how we differ with others in our thinking and behavior, we cannot allow such differences to keep us from cooperating with them in any socially helpful purpose. "I refuse to serve on a committee with him because I do not like his religion, or his political affiliation, or some of the personal habits that he practices from day to day." If people said exactly what they think, wouldn't this be a familiar statement?

Think how progress would have been hindered if God had taken such an attitude toward the leaders he had to work with. Moses, one of the greatest men in history, was far from being perfect. When he saw one of his people mistreated by an Egyptian slavemaster, he showed his temper as he fought with the assailant. Yet the Lord looked past the human weakness displayed by Moses, found his good qualities, and used him as a leader in establishing the Gospel of Jesus Christ among his people.

The Apostle Paul seemed to have a hard time living up to his ideals. He became so angry at times that he spoke cross words and acted like a cantankerous child. Under the withering effects of personal persecution, he found it difficult to maintain his faith and love his enemies. It was just about all he could do to be patient with the old conservative Jews who criticized his teachings. Even after he had been converted to Christ, it is interesting to note, Paul's faults were still with him. "The good that I would, I do not: but the evil which I would not, that I do." (Romans 7:19.) If the Lord had refused to work with Paul because of his weakness, the work of the kingdom would have been greatly retarded.

One day Jesus' disciples came to him, saying, "Master, we saw one casting out devils in thy name; and we forbade him, because he followeth not with us. And Jesus said . . . Forbid him not: for he that is not against us is for us." (Luke 9:49-50.) The Savior was simply asking which was better—to contend with others because of some small difference in ideals or methods, or to forget these differences and contend together against some big problem or evil?

Because no two people have exactly the same ideas and ideals and habits of behavior, the man who refuses to cooperate with others because they see and feel and act contrary to his own convictions will find it necessary to walk alone. No doubt, Jesus would have approved of the way one group of people handled their differences. Though they disagreed among themselves radically at times, they were able to work together successfully. "We have agreed to differ and have placed the emphasis not on the fact that we differ, but on the fact that we have agreed. In other words, we have *agreed* to differ." Christ would have liked the motto, "Agree to differ; resolve to love, and unite so serve."

Why do we sometimes walk alone?

Thus far we have seen that Christ-like courtesy means, in the first place, looking beyond class distinction and recognizing the potential worth of every individual. In the second place, it means a willingness to be sympathetic with individual differences and to search beneath such differences for common purposes and ideals with which we can wholeheartedly cooperate. We go a step farther in Christlike courtesy when we develop such a deep respect for one as a human soul that even when he turns upon us as an enemy and refuses to acknowledge the existence and the value of our common ideals, we still try to appreciate his point of view.

We thrill at the words of Christ on the cross, "Father, forgive them." But we sometimes forget that the remaining words of the sentence are also important: "Father, forgive them; *for they know not what they do.*" (Luke 23:34.) His crucifiers saw with the eyes of cruel Roman law instead of with the vision of Christian sympathy and brotherhood. Knowing this, Jesus, instead of hating them, could pity them and feel sorry for their ignorance.

Tolstoy was once caught by a group of bandits and robbed of everything he had on his person. When the bandits finally released him, they said with curiosity, "You are the strangest man that we have ever seen. We take everything from you and mistreat you, and still you show no sign of anger."

"Why should I be angry?" asked Tolstoy. "I am sorry to lose my goods, but I think I understand why you have taken them. I was reared to believe that life is something more than material things. And as I was taught also that he who takes from another without right, wrongs none so much as himself. It is evident to me now that you have had no such training. Instead you have been lead to believe the way to get the most out of life is to take all that you can from others. Do I not get much more out of my life because of my training? Why should I hate you because of your weakness?"

Can it not be truthfully said of the bandits as was said of the persecutors of Jesus, "they know not what they do"? They knew that they were stealing, but the history of their past lives made impossible a true understanding of their deed.

In the words of Rutledge, "We have all gone off the gold standard, but a human being of integrity and courtesy will always be worth his weight in gold. . . . High courage that bequeaths to all mankind its infinite estate, gaiety that sings on the lonely road, courtesy that thinks of the other person first—are not these and a multitude of other virtues as constant in their value as fine gold?"

Jesus exemplified these virtues and believed it was possible for us to achieve them. He had faith in the worst of men because he had caught the vision of the possible best in mankind.

REFLECTIONS ON FAITH AND PRAYER

The prospects are as bright as the promises of God.

—ADONIRAM JUDSON

Keep your face toward the sunshine, and the shadows will fall behind you.

—WALT WHITMAN

Someday people will learn that material things do not bring happiness and are of little use in making men and women creative and powerful. Then the scientists of the world will turn their laboratories over to the study of God, prayer, and to the spiritual forces which as yet have hardly been guessed at. When that day comes, the world will see more advancement in one generation than it has in the past four.

—DR. CHARLES R. STEINMETZ

Even a strong man cannot lift himself.

—ANONYMOUS

'Tis looking down that makes one dizzy.

—BROWNING

If a person spends sixteen hours a day dealing with things and five minutes a day trying to find God, it will not be strange if things seem two hundred times as real as God.

—DEAN INGE

CHAPTER XI

HAVE FAITH IN GOD

What are the advantages of faith? Is there any proof that we may obtain these advantages? How can we express our faith in such a way as to secure them?

"Keep your face toward the sunshine."

While these questions may seem a selfish approach to the principle of faith and its place in our lives, I consider them without apology; for although the Lord admonished us to think more of others than of self—although he told his followers to be the salt of the earth, the light of the world and the servant of all—he also promised some very definite and specific returns to the individual who observes the principles that he taught.

Jesus did not speak of his Father as an over-indulgent giver. He did not promise riches in return for righteous living. This great teacher, the Savior of the world, lived in a mud house, surrounded by the barest necessities, and had only the most meager meals and the plainest clothes; he never even hinted that God his Father would send us, his children on earth, beautiful mansions, expensive cars, and luxurious food and clothing. He did proclaim that a person who obeys the laws of God will receive the rewards that such laws promise.

While our Father may not be an over-indulgent giver, I cannot imagine his angels looking over the parapet of heaven and doling out headaches to those who refuse to obey his laws. A person who will not work in accordance with the laws will receive the punishment affixed to such carelessness or stubbornness. Should a driver forget to fill his automobile tank with gasoline, he will soon find himself walking instead of riding. Eat too many hot dogs and pain results. Take proper care of one's body and belongings, and (barring unforeseen interferences) health and prosperity will follow.

The principles that Jesus revealed operate in much the same fashion, in accord with law. Be merciful and you will obtain mercy. Give service and you will receive better service in return. And if we have faith, because of the very nature of God's world, we are certain to get results that could not be obtained without it. No mystery hovers about the principle; life is simply made that way. And the sooner we realize it, the more practical our life and religion will become.

Most of us have read the wonderful words of our Savior to his disciples, or have at least attended a funeral where they have been quoted. "Let not your heart be troubled: ye believe in God, believe also in me. In my Father's house are many mansions: if it were not so, I would have told you." (John 14:1-2.) This passage has special significance for Latter-day Saints, particularly for the aged and for all who stand near the edge of life.

A short time ago I called on an elderly woman who was so seriously ill that I wondered if any words or blessings of mine could be of help. For the past six months she had been completely paralyzed from her waist down and had enjoyed only the slightest use of her hands. I was a perfect stranger coming to visit her at the request of her granddaughter. As I neared the bedside, she smiled and extended her shaking hand to me, showing not the faintest sign of sorrow. In fact, she was so very optimistic that I soon found myself joking with her and laughing in turn at some of the thoughts and ideas she shared from her past experiences. Did this sweet sister realize that she would probably never rise again from her sick bed? Yes, but she was so thoroughly convinced of her relationship with her Heavenly Father that she had no reason to worry about the future.

From her room, I went to that of another wonderful person, a man some ten years younger than she. He had been kept on his back for several months because of a severe stroke. The doctors had allowed him only slight movements of his arms and legs. As we talked for a while, he told me with no sign of bitterness that he thought the end was near and asked me to give him a special blessing. As I left his side, I thanked the Lord for the faith that could lead men and women to the very doors of death with a smile on their faces and a hope in their hearts.

To one who faces tragedy, a sincere faith in God is most precious and helpful. However, most of us are not constantly confronted with tragedy. We still have dreams we expect to realize. We still arise from our beds in the morning with a determination to conquer an enemy and win some new victory. And if we are young enough, we plan to do impossible things which no other person has ever done. Not very much interested at the present in how to die successfully, we want to know how to live victoriously. Is there not something in the teachings of the Savior that can challenge such people?

Jesus would have us know that strong, true faith can help us gain everything our divine Father thinks we need. Is it exotic food and expensive clothes that we really need? From Christ's challenge to his disciples we can draw wise counsel for our own lives. "Take no thought for your life, what ye shall eat, or what ye shall drink; nor yet for your body, what ye shall put on." (Matt. 6:25, and 3 Nephi 13:25.) He is not saying we ought not to exert our best talents. He merely says that we should not be overly anxious about our material possessions; there is another non-material facet of life and of our being which needs nourishment and care. Our Heavenly Father is already aware of our physical needs. In the same verse of scripture the Savior points out, "Is not the life more than meat, and the body than raiment?" Why worry about that which holds, or should hold, a secondary place in our lives?

Jesus taught that we can do what is generally con-

Where do you sparkle?

sidered impossible if we have sufficient faith. Do you remember the story of the old woman who prayed to God to remove a mountain from in front of her house? When she arose the next morning and saw the mountain still there, she said impatiently, "Just as I expected!" While there is no doubt that the Savior or anyone else with sufficient faith properly exercised could literally move mountains, Jesus also taught that if we would work hard enough with pick, shovel, and truck, having a strong belief in the power of systematized work, we would ourselves move the mountain to another place. It requires, as James has suggested, faith plus works. (James 2: 14-26.)

To show how powerful faith can be in a person's life, Jesus compared it to the smallest amount the Jews could easily think of, a tiny mustard seed, and using a forceful figure of speech he indicated that this small amount could be victorious over even the largest difficulties. "If ye have faith as a grain of mustard seed, ye shall say unto this mountain, Remove hence to yonder place; and it shall remove; and nothing shall be impossible unto you." (Matt. 17:20.) Apparently, what Jesus intended them and and us to understand is the truth that faith and the power of faith can literally not be measured. What man with his finite knowledge considers impossible, faith in the infinite power can accomplish, if, of course, it is in accordance with the will of God. "With God all things are possible." (Matt. 19:26.) Or, as one returned missionary said to me recently, "There is nothing that lies outside the power of prayer, save that which lies outside the power of God."

Have we any proof that faith will bring such advantages, success in our labors and the realization of our dreams? In the *Age of Reason*, Thomas Payne attempted to show the foolishness of faith. Just as extreme, but to the other end of the scale, Luther Bacon spoke this way of faith: "The more incredible a thing is, the more honor I do God in believing it." But is faith such a strange and vacuous abstraction that no one can understand it or find a reasonable explanation for its existence?

The Lord himself found a source of faith in the beauty of his creations. Can anyone look at waving fields of grain, at flowery hillsides, at sparkling streams and rugged mountains and contend that nature is not beautiful? Even the richest clothes of a king's wardrobe, wonderful in style and gorgeous in color as they may be, cannot begin to compare with the beauty of nature. Admitting the hand of a great Creator in the scheme of things, would it not seem strange on the basis of pure logic alone for God our Heavenly Father and his Son Jesus Christ to give us such gifts of beauty but refuse to help us in the attainment of our needs? "If God so clothe the grass of the field, which today is, and tomorrow is cast into the oven, shall he not much more clothe you, O ye of little faith?" (Matt. 6:30, and 3 Nephi 13:30.) This is not poetry; it is plain logical reasoning on the part of the Master.

Stepping up from the world of nature, for another comparison Jesus spoke of the shepherd's sympathetic concern and care for his sheep. All day long the shepherd tends his wandering sheep, searching for green pastures and cool waters that they may have refreshment, calling them back to the safety of the fold when they are tempted to go astray, protecting them at the risk of his own life from the jaws of hungry, wild animals, rubbing oil on their wounds when they are injured, taking them into his arms and loving them when they are tired, and when night comes on and he finds that one of them has lost its way, going from the fold to seek it out and bring it safely home. (See Psalm 23 and Luke 15:4.)

Is this concern of the shepherd entirely commercial? Evidently the author of the twenty-third Psalm did not think so. Knowing the secrets of shepherd life and the care of the shepherd for his sheep, the psalmist wrote, "The Lord is my shepherd; I shall not want." (Psalm 23:1.) Similarly, the Savior certainly had no materialistic concept in mind when he compared himself and his Father to the good shepherd. One who has worked with animals for any length of time knows how lonesome he feels when separated from them. The sheep in their distress need the shepherd, but the shepherd also needs the sheep.

If that be true in the relationship of human beings

and lower animals, how much truer would it be in the relationship between a Father-Creator and the children of his creation! Without his love and care, our lives can never be fully satisfied; and without our reverence and devotion to him, his own being cannot be complete.

Jesus went still another step higher. Seeing a young boy in the multitude eating a piece of bread, this Master Teacher asked the lad's father why he had given the boy the bread. Why not a stone? There were plenty of stones on the ground.

I recently asked a former student of mine who had just returned from a six-week tour of Palestine what made the deepest impression on his mind as he traveled over the sacred country. Without hesitation he responded, "Stones, stones, stones! Almost every place you look in Palestine, you see what appears to be millions of them." The story is told that during the creation of the world, the angel whose business it was to distribute stones over the earth slipped and fell before he had finished the job. The sack ripped open and nearly all the stones were left in the land of Palestine.

With this picture in mind, we can better appreciate the Savior's visual aid and his question, "What man is there of you, whom, if his son ask bread, will he give him a stone? Or if he ask a fish, will he give him a serpent?" (Matt. 7:9-19, and 3 Nephi 14:9-10.) There is our answer. And there is the logic of faith, which no one has ever successfully refuted. The man had given the boy a piece of bread instead of a stone because the boy was his son.

What volumes are written in that single phrase! Unless mothers and fathers are very abnormal, they love their sons and daughters with such intensity that they will do almost anything within their power to keep their children from suffering. It is so not only in Palestine—in any particular country—or in any state of the union; it is an almost universal fact that parents so love their children, that if necessary they would give their lives to save them. Could one want proof—more proof—of the love of an eternal Father for us?

Can the thing created be greater than its creator? If we as parents have such intense devotion for our children, would it not seem reasonable to suppose that the Divine Power which created us would have at least an equal amount of love within himself? And if that love, out of which he has created us, is no greater than the love we have for our children, that should be enough to assure us proper care.

I emphasize again, as did the Savior, the logic of the situation. Would a Creator give us such beauties in nature for our enjoyment and use but refuse to go a step farther to help us in a time of need? Would he put into the shepherd's heart such sacrificial consideration for his sheep, would he give the fathers and mothers throughout the world such intense love for their children, if he himself had not at least an equal portion of this spirit of love in his heart for us? One can hardly create something greater than himself.

How, then, shall we gain the advantages of faith? The answer is so simple that it surprises us when we finally discover it; yet it is so difficult to put into practice that very few of us ever learn the fullness of its meaning. Jesus told us that if we have the right kind of faith, if we are careful to give it proper expression, we can have anything the Father feels we need. After giving several strong arguments to support his message that God will abundantly reward the faithful, Christ opened to us in a few simple words the secret of faith's expression. "If ye abide in me, and my words abide in you"— no, he does not say anything about beautiful prayers or the payment of debts or the number of times we attend church services, but—"If ye abide in me, and my words abide in you, ye shall *ask what ye will, and it shall be done unto you.*" (John 15:7. Italics added.)

The great answer.

Simple, yes? But what does he mean by the statement "abide in me"? Picture in your mind two young people, each going his own separate way, each doing as he pleases with particular consideration for anyone else, each interested in his own affairs, and each determined to be his own master. But love comes their way, and in due process of time the two become one. Must the young man sign a contract or must the young lady make a written promise before each will believe the other?

Does one still follow his own way without thought of his sweetheart? Not if they really abide in each other, not if they are truly one. So long as love is their master, they live as though they were one mind and one heart.

Jesus illustrates the same idea of unity by a vine and its branches. "I am the vine, ye are the branches: He that abideth in me, and I in him, the same bringeth forth much fruit: for without me ye can do nothing." (John 15:5.) How can we obtain that which our Heavenly Father feels we need? *Abide in him.* Let our hopes be his hopes, let our aspirations for ourselves and for the work we do for others be his aspirations. Let us endeavor so to think his thoughts and so to do his will that in very truth it will be no longer "we" who live, but the Christ that dwelleth in us, directing our plans and assuring our purposes.

Perhaps you have heard, as have I, many people tell about the failures of their lives—until they finally decided to give themselves completely to the service of their fellowmen. I recall only a short while ago one such associate of mine who said, "And from that day until this, I have been able to work longer hours, to make better plans, and to be more successful in the accomplishment of my plans than ever before." These people have not used some magic formula. They have simply followed our Savior's suggestion that one align his hopes with the hopes of God our Father.

The logic of the situation seems perfectly clear. If, as Paul tells us, it is in God that we live and move and have our being (Acts 17:28), the more we surrender to his purpose and plan and open our minds and hearts to him, the more he can give his way to our lives. The adage, "Let go and let God," is wise advice. But it is of little value unless we are willing to follow both halves of it. To say "let God" is useless unless we are willing at the same time to let go of selfish ambitions and self-centered fears.

Speaking of God's relationship to the human race, a great teacher once said, "He loves every one of us as though there were but one of us to love." That is true of human parents. Why should it not be true of the one great Eternal Father, who made such love possible in the hearts of mortal fathers and mothers? Jesus pleads with us, "Let not your heart be troubled: ye believe in God, believe also in me." (John 14:1.) "Take no thought for your life, what ye shall eat, or what ye shall drink; nor yet for your body, what ye shall put on. . . . But seek ye first the kingdom of God, and his righteousness; and all these things shall be added unto you." (Matt. 6:25, 33, and 3 Nephi 13: 25, 33.) "Ask, and it shall be given you, seek, and ye shall find; knock, and it shall be opened unto you." (Matt. 7:7, and 3 Nephi 14:7.) "All things, whatsoever ye shall ask in prayer, believing, ye shall receive." (Matt. 21:22.)

REFLECTION ON BEING DOERS

Let us endeavor so to live that when we come to die even the undertaker will be sorry.

—MARK TWAIN

I desire mercy, and not sacrifice; and the knowledge of God more than burnt offerings.

—HOS. 6:6

What doeth the Lord require of thee, but to do justly, and to love mercy, and to walk humbly with thy God.

—MICAH 6:8

CHAPTER XII

BE YE DOERS

To many who do not understand fully the gospel of Jesus Christ the question as to which comes first, the chicken or the egg, is still a problem. Theologians are still debating which is first in the development of a strong life, belief or action. In the meantime, hens continue to lay eggs and eggs continue to produce chickens, to the profit of farmers and the public at large. And when we

Which comes first?

become as wise in our religious thinking as we are in our farming we shall appreciate much more than we do now the close relationship existing between our faith and our deeds.

On the one side of the problem, James tells us, "Faith, if it hath not works, is dead." (James 2:17.) Do we say that we believe ideals are more important than money? If we cheat a man to make a dollar, or if we are unfair to our employer or employee, we show that we do not believe what we have professed. We say we believe ideals are more important than material things. But if we give so much of our time to business that we have little or no time left for our home life and for the cultivation of religious faith in the life of our children, we are simply playing a trick on ourselves.

We contend that form is not nearly so important as fellowship, but if we fight with each other in our wards and stakes and in our political parties to gain a certain type of organization, or if we insist upon judging the orthodoxy of other people by their religious views or their political theories instead of by their works, we show clearly that we do not really believe that we have professed.

This is what James meant when he said, "Faith, if it hath not works, is dead." That is what Jesus undoubtedly had in mind when he said that men were judged by their fruits. "Therefore whosoever hearth these sayings of mine, and doeth them, I will liken him unto a wise man, which built his house upon a rock." (Matt. 7:24, and 3 Nephi 14:24.) This does not refer to a raised foundation such as we have in the United States. In Palestine they dug below the shifting surface to find solid rock. And when a house is built upon the hard foundation, even though the rains descend and the floods come and the winds blow and beat upon it, it does not shift from its location.

"And every one that heareth these sayings of mine, and doeth them not, shall be likened unto a foolish man, which built his house upon the sand: and the rain descended and the floods came, and the winds blew, and smote upon that house; and it fell: and great was the fall of it." (Matt. 7:26-27, and 3 Nephi 14:26-27.) Whether it be a material building or a spiritual faith it is certain to slip and fall away unless it is substantially grounded. With a house it is a rock beneath the surface: with faith it is conscientious action.

Again we hear the Master warn his hearers against the fault of thinking that orthodoxy and belief will save them in the days to come. On the judgment day he will ask if they have believed in feeding the hungry. Emphatically yes!" Then perhaps they can give the names of some of the people whom they have fed. They contend that they had a strong faith in the value of human kindness and sympathy. Very well, then let them tell about some of the lonesome people they have visited. No use to call him, "Lord, Lord" unless they have been willing to do what he has asked them to do. Orthodoxy or belief means little without the orthodoxy of good works. (Matt. 7:21, and 3 Nephi 14:21.)

In discussing this passage one might well ask: By what code of law and by what standard shall we be judged on judgement day? Here is a possible answer: "Not by creeds and church questions, but by our human efforts; by the reality of our inner feelings; by our solidarity with our fellowmen. If we lived in the presence of hunger, loneliness, oppression, in the same neighborhood with those who are less fortunate, in a community with social evils, political injustices — if we saw such things and remained apathetc and indifferent, out we go."

I think one of the best pictures in the New Testament to bring out this principle is that contained in the Savior's Sermon on the Mount. "Ye shall know them by their fruits. Do men gather grapes of thorns, or figs of thistles? Even so every good tree bringeth forth good fruit; but a corrupt tree bringeth forth evil fruit. A good tree cannot bring forth evil fruit, neither can a corrupt tree bring forth good fruit. Every tree that bringeth not forth good fruit is hewn down, and cast into the fire. Wherefore by their fruits ye shall know them." (Matt. 7:16-20, 3 Nephi 14:16-20.)

John the Baptist, in teaching his followers, put it this way, "And now also the axe is laid unto the root of the trees: therefore every tree which bringeth not forth good fruit is hewn down, and cast into the fire. And think not to say within yourselves, We have Abraham to our father: for I say unto you, that God is able of these stones to raise up children unto Abraham." (Matt. 3:10, 9.)

It does not make any difference who our ancestors are, what race we belong to, or how much church or political influence is doing for the welfare of our brother. It may be that a person's wife, or husband, or children, are actively engaged in some unselfish work in the Church or community. Even that does not make any difference. The thing that John the Baptist has in mind and the question that Jesus is constantly concerned about is how much you and I as individuals — apart from any relationship we may hold in the Church, nation, or family — are doing for the building of the kingdom of God. Are we using our abilities for our own sakes, or are we actively being useful to those about us? Not matter how correct our beliefs may be, unless we are at least attempting to bear fruit for God and man we are wasting valuable space in a dependent society.

A doctor friend of mine often puts it this way, when talking to a patient about the necessity of exercising his muscles: "You either use them or lose them." No amount of medicine or good food or alibis will turn the trick alone. According to the law of muscles, as with everything else in life, you either "use them or lose them." I remember reading a pamphlet which showed the costs of progress in the business world. It told of one manufacturing establishment that spent several million dollars in machinery that would produce a certain expensive article, only to find after installing the machinery that another company had discovered a way of producing the same article at a much lower cost. Of course there was only one thing for the first company to do. Since its machinery could not be used successfully against such competition the manufacturer had to put it aside.

When you cannot use a thing advantageously you lose it. When John and James and Jesus enunciated this principle of action they were not talking about something that was peculiar to religion only. They were simply emphasizing a law of life. The thing that cannot pass a pragmatic test soon dies. If faith does not work, it passes away. If one hears and does not obey and if one professes great belief and does not do great things, it is a sign that there is no faith worth mentioning. "You either use them or lose them." "Even so faith, if it hath not works, is dead." (James 2:17.)

Use them or lose them.

In ancient Palestine it was common practice to pay a tax on every tree that stood on the land, fruitful or not. Because they did not want to pay taxes on trees that did not bear fruit, owners of orchards were careful to cut down all unproductive timber. The question might well be asked, "Is the Church today paying unnecessary taxes on a lot of dead wood?" Permit me to suggest a few simple cases.

A young professional man who was investigating the Church told me on one occasion he had decided to join the faith. When I congratulated him on his decision he informed me that although he did not feel any real need for the gospel, he thought it might pay him professionally to have contact with a group of such influential people. "Besides, it will not cost the Church much to have me on its rolls even though I am only a partially active member."

It will not cost the Church to have him as an inactive member? Yet, every time a bishop or home teacher or a quorum leader tries to teach or reach him and attempts to challenge the people of his ward to accept a worthwhile project of helpfulness, this lazy member stands as a silent example denying the validity of the gospel message. And what a tax the Church must pay upon that influence!

In a community where I once lived there were two women in a ward choir who by their action decided not to love each other. They were good people and well respected in the community. They believed in God. They accepted Jesus Christ and they enjoyed the work of the Church. But every time one was asked to serve in any capacity or to do any kind of work for the Church she refused, if she thought the other one had been included. And the Church, because of this continuous fight, was unable to accomplish its full quota of work. Did it not pay a tremendous tax on the enmity of these two people?

Not long ago I was talking to a group of young high school students. After I had given them the best talk that

I could prepare on the evils of drinking and taking into their bodies certain kinds of poisonous material, and when I thought that I almost had them to the point of accepting my message, one of the young men asked me: "Did you know that Mr. ...., our principal, drinks quite often?"

"No," I said, "I had not been conscious of that fact."

"Well," said the young man, "he does follow this little custom quite frequently and of course you know and I know that he is the top official in this school." The boys all laughed, and for the rest of the period endeavored to shoot holes in my argument. Did not this school pay a tax on the harmful habits of Mr. ...., the principal?

I remember that the Apostle Paul was willing, even though he probably enjoyed meat very much and saw not the slightest personal harm in eating that which had been placed as an offering before idols, to refrain from eating a single bite of meat as long as the world stood—if and when the eating of such food could be found to have a harmful influence upon his fellowmen. Such teaching reaches a higher water mark in the field of ethics. But being a Christ-like disciple means living on the highest possible level. And the Church pays a heavy tax on the influence of every member who is not willing to do his best to walk on this high ground.

A few years ago I asked a large number of college students assembled in a religious emphasis week assembly how many of them attended Sunday School classes. When only a few answered in the affirmative I asked the others why they did not go; and I was somewhat surprised to hear them say that it was because the average Sunday School teacher of their experience ·had so little to give them. "Public school teachers and college professors spend years in preparing for their particular fields, and, in addition, give hours of study for a single lesson. Do you expect us to sit under church teachers who know little more about the subject than those they are trying to teach?" Regardless of the cause of this condition, is it not clear that their churches were paying a tremendous tax on the inefficiency — and in many cases the carelessness — of its lay leadership?

This is only one side of the picture. The Church has some workers on whom it will never be compelled to pay a tax. Note the case of a certain young man of my acquaintance who had taught a class of boys every Tuesday evening for several years. A friend had knocked on his door one Tuesday evening and said, "I have come to give you a much-coveted birthday present. I know how anxious you are to see the St. Louis Cardinals play the Dodgers, and since this is your birthday I am here tonight to take you to that choice game."

"Oh, that's great. I will be with you in a minute," said the young man. "Just wait until I get my coat." And in a moment he returned, jubilantly excited. But as he walked out of the house and closed the door he suddenly stopped and said, "Good heavens I can't do it!"

"You can't do it! Why, man you're crazy! This is the thing you have been waiting for for months."

"No," said the young man, "I've just remembered this is Tuesday. I can't go tonight, for I am teaching a class of boys at Mutual and it's almost time for me to go to my assignment."

"But it won't hurt to miss class for one week. You can easily get someone else to take your place."

"Yes," said the young man, "I could get a substitute, I suppose, but it would be impossible for me to make these boys believe that I considered them important, that I thought much of my religion, if I should give up my responsibility even for a choice ball game that comes around only once in a great while."

No program will ever pay a tax on a man like that.

Now the question arises, how can we get faith sufficient to do great work? Jesus replies, "If any man will do [God's] will, he shall know." (John 7:17.) Faith, if it is of the proper sort, will eventuate in action; and action, if it is the right kind, will produce faith. So true is this that it is difficult to know which comes first in the process. At least we can be assured that you cannot separate faith from action.

I recall an incident in the life of a former colleague of mine. He tells a story of a man who came into his office one day with a statement that he intended to take his own life.

"All right," said my friend, "go ahead. But before you take your life I want you to do me one favor." My friend then told him of a very poor home where the mother was ill and the children were in need of much help. He asked the man if he would go to this home and as a last gesture offer them what help they needed. The directions were followed. The man did everything he could to provide food, clothing, and the other necessities of life for the family. A few years later he appeared again in the presence of my friend, and said; "Your plan worked. I am able to dispose of my life in the life of my fellowmen. The faith which I tried to argue into my mind came at last through service."

A pretty good picture, it seems to me, of one of Christ's divine principles. Mental arguments are often cold. Words are seldom enough to paint the joy of sacrificial living and the glory of unlimited faith in our Heavenly Father.

This principle of service should suggest to us as individuals the unlimited opportunities for faith building that lie withn our power. Do we believe as we should like to believe? Does the appeal of the spiritual world seem as strong as we wish it were? Do we try to give logical arguments for being more idealistic and yet find it difficult to sacrifice as we should for the attainment of great ideals? Perhaps the fact is that we have not experimented enough with the faith we have. It has not grown because we have not given it sufficient exercise. We have not plunged into the deep water. We have not taken chances with God. We have not been willing to gamble our soul

Faith without works is dead.

against "the mess of pottage." We are thinking too much and not acting enough. Of course we must not try to build a religion devoid of reasoning. But it is just as foolish to attempt a religious faith by reason alone. "Faith, if it hath not works, is dead." (James 2:17) "If any man will do his will, he shall know of the doctrine." (John 7:17.)

In summary, Jesus said that:

If one will exercise the spirit of meekness, one shall inherit the earth. (But let us remember that the biggest value in the earth, according to the Savior's philosophy of life, are not found in material things.)

If one will work as hard for righteousness as he works to satisfy physical hunger and thirst, he shall be filled— with the Holy Ghost.

If he will show mercy (not if he merely thinks about it), he shall obtain mercy.

If he will do pure, unmuddied thinking, he shall see God.

If he will always try to make peace, he shall be listed among the "children of God."

If he will meet trouble with a smile and endeavor to use it constructively, it shall prove a blessing instead of a burden. By serving others one also serves God and himself to the best advantage.

One loses and others lose when one becomes tempestuous; but every worthy person concerned will profit when one is tempered to fight injustices in our social order.

Only simple honesty, a fearless facing of every truth, can make for stability and harmony in individual life and in the life of the world at large.

In its battle with jealousy and hatred, love always wins in the long run.

Sincere courtesy, aside from being deserved by others, will generally rebound with an extra supply of courtesy for ourselves.

Only as one learns the joy of forgetting self and proving a help and a blessing to others can he know what it means to be truly great.

Could one ask more of any leader than Jesus' promise to us? We do not have to be good just to please him or to satisfy an intolerant Father. We are to follow his advice because, as the Savior of mankind has indicated, he knows and has been able to tell us in simple, common-sense language how to hit the center of the target of life. Disregard his teachings and we miss the mark. Follow him and, as surely as the sun rises tomorrow and the seasons come in their turn, we shall experience both here and in the hereafter the joy of an abundant eternal life.

A CODE FOR LATTER-DAY SAINT LIVING

1. *Be Humble* — Keep your mind open — your energies properly focused.

2. *Be Courteous* — Not only concerning the social graces but spiritual courtesy as well.

3. *Be Merciful — Tolerant* — Do unto others — the golden rule. "Greater love hath no man than this."

4. *Be Honest* — Not only with others and the world but with yourselves.

5. *Be Practical — Balance* — In all things — your home, business and church.

6. *Be Courageous* — In your religion as well as in the face of fear and danger.

7. *Live Helpfully* — Love your neighbor as yourself — non-Mormons and Mormons alike.

8. *Help Others to Find Peace* — Civic and community responsibilities. Spiritual as well as mental and physical.

9. *Control Your Temper* — In all things.

10. *Be Pure* — In mind as well as in body.

11. *Be Righteous* — Living your religion all 24 hours of the day.

12. *Have Faith and Trust in God* — Testimony of Christ and of the Church.